Life-Changing Cross-Cultural Friendships is a practical application of Kingdom Race Theology. It provides doable steps, helping Christians go beyond reading or talking about race relations to tangible acts to make a lasting difference for unity in the world in which we live.

—Dr. Tony Evans, senior pastor, Oak Cliff Bible Fellowship; founder and president, Urban Alternative

Very grateful to have people exercise humility and grace to dive into this conversation in a healthy way. This book will be helpful for many.

—Lecrae, Grammy Award–winning artist

Recently, I've asked several Black brothers and sisters, "How do I help with the racial division in our country?" Without exception, their response has included the pursuit of interracial friendships. Even with the best of intentions, this advice goes unheeded if we don't know how to navigate the barriers and potential triggers in such relationships. Gary and Clarence's book is sensitive, compelling, and informative in spelling out the how. Its advice and example will do much to heal the wounds of the Western church, one relationship at a time.

—Juli Slattery, PsyD, president and cofounder, Authentic Intimacy

No scolding, no guilt trips, just powerful reminders and solid counsel on how to start healing the rifts between cultures. Eschewing the cliché of pretending colorblindness, Drs. Chapman and Shuler have learned to appreciate and love each other. I feel honored to call Gary and Clarence friends.

—Jerry B. Jenkins, bestselling author; founder, Jerry Jenkins Writers Guild

Gary Chapman and Clarence Shuler require no introduction. Their decades of groundbreaking work speak for themselves. I'm thankful that God has led them to bring their expertise into the sphere of cross-cultural, multiracial relationships. In a world marked by racial division and political upheaval, Chapman and Shuler's voices guide people of faith back to the foundation of the gospel and the love of Christ, which breaks all cultural barriers and acknowledges the differences that make us unique image-bearers of God.

—Samuel Rodriguez, lead pastor, New Season; president and CEO, NHCLC; author, *Persevere with Power* and *What Heaven Starts, Hell Cannot Stop!*; executive producer, *Breakthrough* and *Flamin' Hot*

In *Life-Changing Cross-Cultural Friendships*, Gary Chapman and Clarence Shuler both beautifully express how to live out the gospel of Jesus Christ in a racially divided world. Through the chapters in this book, they show how to overcome hurdles through establishing relationships of trust, authenticity, respect, sacrifice, honor, friendship, and commitment. Ultimately, they reflect "a friend who sticks closer than a brother," our creator and reconciler, Jesus Christ!

—Huron Claus, president and CEO, CHIEF, Inc., a ministry to Native American people

I have never met these authors, but I have been in conversation with Clarence Shuler for many years. I trust these brothers, and I highly recommend their work. They are living what they write. Trust them and learn how to become effective agents of reconciliation in this divided world.

—William Pannell, emeritus professor of preaching, Fuller Theological Seminary; author, *The Coming Race Wars: A Cry for Justice, from Civil Rights to Black Lives Matter*

Forty years ago, I became a US citizen, embracing all the goodness, corruption, and racism of this country. As a Latino in the USA married to a Chinese, I understand the challenges of living across cultures. I was truly touched by this book; specifically, I found the lists of different types of friendships helpful and I was educated by the steps outlined to create cross-cultural friendships. This book has taught me important ways I can narrow the differences that exist in my world.

—Wolfgang D. Fernández, global citizen; NextGen mentor; HeartCore changer

When confronted with profoundly complex problems and crises, sometimes the most important step is the initial one. Gary Chapman and Clarence Shuler offer an example of the necessary first step in the journey toward healing in our world. The power of friendship that embodies the important work of Christian witness and God's justice is demonstrated in a beautiful and real way through the story of these two individuals.

—Soong-Chan Rah, Robert Munger Professor of Evangelism, Fuller Theological Seminary; author, *The Next Evangelicalism* and *Prophetic Lament*

Life-Changing
Cross-Cultural
Friendships

Life-Changing
Cross-Cultural
Friendships

HOW YOU CAN HELP HEAL
RACIAL DIVIDES,
ONE RELATIONSHIP AT A TIME

GARY CHAPMAN &
CLARENCE SHULER

ZONDERVAN BOOKS

Life-Changing Cross-Cultural Friendships
Copyright © 2022 by Gary Chapman and Clarence Shuler

Requests for information should be addressed to:
Zondervan, *3900 Sparks Dr. SE, Grand Rapids, Michigan 49546*

Zondervan titles may be purchased in bulk for educational, business, fundraising, or sales
promotional use. For information, please email SpecialMarkets@Zondervan.com.

ISBN 978-0-310-36503-7 (audio)

Library of Congress Cataloging-in-Publication Data

Names: Chapman, Gary D., 1938- author. | Shuler, Clarence, author.
Title: Life-changing cross-cultural friendships : how you can help heal racial divides, one
    relationship at a time / Gary Chapman, Clarence Shuler.
Description: Grand Rapids : Zondervan, 2022. | Includes bibliographical references. |
    Summary: "After decades of knowing each other, bestselling author Gary Chapman and
    counselor and diversity trainer Dr. Clarence Shuler have come to believe that if each of
    us formed Life-Changing Cross-Cultural Friendships, it would radically transform race
    relations in our country—and it all starts with you making one new friend"—Provided
    by publisher.
Identifiers: LCCN 2021061614 (print) | LCCN 2021061615 (ebook) | ISBN 9780310365013
    (trade paperback) | ISBN 9780310365020 (ebook)
Subjects: LCSH: Friendship. | Intercultural communication. | Interracial friendship. | Social
    exchange. | Interpersonal relations.
Classification: LCC HM1161 .C43 2022 (print) | LCC HM1161 (ebook) | DDC 302--dc23/
    eng/20220202
LC record available at https://lccn.loc.gov/2021061614
LC ebook record available at https://lccn.loc.gov/2021061615

Cover design: Studio Gearbox
Cover photo: Rawpixel.com / Shutterstock
Interior design: Sara Colley

Printed in the United States of America

22 23 24 25 26 27 28 29 30 31 32 /LSC/ 15 14 13 12 11 10 9 8 7 6 5 4 3 2 1

To Gloria and Rodger Henn

In 2008, Gloria Henn said, "Gary Chapman and you should write a book about your friendship. I think it would help so many people to work to have healthy cross-cultural friendships and lower racism in America. Your friendship would be a model for them."

Gloria and Rodger, her husband, have worked so diligently and long to improve race relations in their city. One year, they visited churches of cultures different from their own and made culturally different friends. They model Christ's love and bring a smile to his face.

Thank you, Gloria and Rodger, for inspiring me as well as giving Gary and me the idea for this book.

Contents

Introduction

What If We Became Friends?

During the summer of 2020, racial tensions in American culture once again made headlines. Images of White policemen killing unarmed African Americans stirred emotions. Our screens were filled with images of individuals breaking windows and looting stores in many of our major cities. On both sides, anger led to overreactions. Some labeled all policemen as racist and called for the abolition of the police.

We believe that most citizens were bewildered that such things could be happening. Many thought that as a nation we were farther along than that in understanding racial differences and learning to live as fellow citizens with respect for all races and cultures. Many were tired and dejected that such things continue to happen to *them*. The August 2019 Walmart shooting in El Paso, Texas, in which twenty-two people were killed, was aimed at Hispanics. During the first quarter of 2021, attacks on Asian Americans spiked by 164 percent, according to police data. And Native Americans experienced the violation of more than eight hundred treaties with the United States government, resulting in massive loss of life, land theft, and the subjection of Native Americans to the power of *American* law.

Many of us have lived long enough to remember the racial tensions that accompanied the integration of schools, restaurants, and other public facilities in the 1960s and '70s. Most Americans saw these changes as a giant step forward in racial relations. Yet here we are, half a century later, appearing to have made little progress in racial understanding.

The obvious question is why. Why have we made so little progress in living together in the United States of America? Where is our unity? And why does it seem so tenuous? We believe it is because we have failed on the interpersonal level in relating to those of a different race or culture. Most Americans do not have a close personal friend of another race. We may have casual acquaintances, but not close friendships.

Some social structural changes, such as school integration, can be legislated. Many of our national and local leaders are seeking to make such changes. But loving relationships cannot be legislated. They must be developed by individuals of different races and cultures. Without deep cross-cultural friendships, we will never understand each other, and our relationships will always be tenuous in America.

As the title reveals, this book is about how you can help heal racial divides one relationship at a time. Cross-cultural friendships become life-changing when we learn from each other, and result in mutually beneficial, intimate, long-lasting relationships while lessening racial tension.

Cross-cultural is not simply a Black-White issue. America

is composed of numerous cultures, all of which deserve to be treated with dignity and respect. We need to develop loving friendships in which we learn from each other and seek to enrich each other's lives. True friends may disagree on many things, but they will not allow disagreements to divide them. They will each seek the well-being of the other. Imagine a nation, and a world, where cross-cultural friendships are a way of life.

We wrote this book together because in the providence of God, our paths crossed and neither of us has ever been the same. We have experienced a deep friendship for more than fifty years. In this book, we share our journey and how our lives have affected each other.

Let us begin by introducing ourselves.

I (Clarence) was born in America to Black parents. Dad and Mom really loved each other. Their love provided a sense of security for me and my sister, Jean. Dad had an eighth-grade education. Mom had a college degree in education. She taught school for a short time, then decided to become a saleswoman in order to make more money. She was an exceptional salesperson, winning trips for our family. We went to places and stayed in hotels that we otherwise could not afford. Dad worked for thirty-eight years as a janitor for a tobacco company. I lived in a segregated community, went to an all-Black church, and attended a segregated school, which I rode to on a segregated public bus. I had no choice in any of these realities.

I (Gary) was born in America to White parents. My mom and dad had a healthy marriage. Neither was highly educated. Both worked in a textile mill. My sister and I always felt safe and loved. I went to a segregated high school and attended an all-White church in a small southern town. I did not choose any of these realities.

In a world often divided by race, it is important to realize that none of us chose our parents, our color, and the place and time of our birth. We were born into a culture which already existed. Some were born into affluent families. Some were born into poverty. Some were born to single moms and never knew their fathers, while others grew up with both a mom and a dad. Some saw their parents divorce, often after experiencing verbal or physical abuse. All of these factors made an impact on our lives.

The Confusion in Racial and Cultural Identity

We acknowledge that there is considerable confusion even in the terms we use when we refer to someone of a different race. For example, would you call me (Gary) White, Caucasian, or Irish American? Would you call me (Clarence) Black, African American, a person of color, or just an American who happens to have black skin? If a person born in Jamaica immigrated to the United States, would we call him or her Black, Jamaican American, African American, or a Black from Jamaica? If you have a friend who is from China or whose parents or ancestors came from China, do you speak of them as your Chinese friend? Or just "my friend Jung"? It is not our purpose to promote a particular term. In building friendships, especially cross-cultural ones, we believe it is essential to use the term that the other person prefers. We also know that derogatory names are sometimes used of various races. These are never appropriate.

Throughout the book, we refer to "racial differences" and "cultural differences." Racial differences have to do with physical distinctives—primarily skin color and facial characteristics. Cultural differences refer to patterned ways of life. For example, Chinese culture is distinct from Indian culture. Culture includes language, family structure, economic system, musical forms, and religion. Of course, within every major culture there are subcultures. For example, we speak of American culture, but we have many subcultures within America. These are ways of life that were brought to America by people from many different cultures. These subcultures operate within the larger framework of American culture. Sometimes we use the words *race* and *culture* interchangeably, but often people of the same race are of different cultures.

According to the latest research, 75 percent of Whites do not have any friends of color, and this percentage is even higher in the evangelical church.[1] If this is your experience, the racial violence and tension in recent years may be new to you. It is, of course, not new to people of color who continue to experience racial violence. But regardless of your racial and cultural experience, one vital message must be shared: building friendships across racial and cultural lines will change individual lives and our country for the better forever.

Interracial contact is inevitable in America, because we are a multicultural country. How we relate to those of another race is a choice. Some choose to largely ignore those who do not look like them. Others choose to acknowledge each other only with a nod and perhaps a "hi." Some, particularly in school and vocational settings, choose to have conversations about work, sports, and the weather. But few have deep and abiding cross-cultural friendships.

Seeking a Biblical Solution to the Racial Divide

We are writing with the deep desire that others might experience friendships across racial and ethnic barriers like we have. We see this as the only hope for eliminating racism from our culture.

I (Clarence) have many friends who don't look like me. I feel that I am rich with friends. Some of my close friends who don't resemble me initially said things that offended me. Some of these friends and I disagree politically. Yet I have found these cross-cultural friendships to be beneficial and life changing. They are valuable and continue to force me to look at situations from a different perspective. They help me process my emotions and reach healthy conclusions. My cross-cultural friends say our relationship does the same for them.

I (Gary) fully agree with Clarence. We don't have to agree on everything to be friends. What is important is that we value each other as persons and desire to understand, encourage, and enrich each other. Clarence and I have had this kind of friendship over many years. We have each experienced the benefits of our friendship. That is why we are so motivated to help others build such relationships.

In this book, in addition to sharing our journey, we will also share the stories of others who have benefited from cross-cultural friendships. We will seek to define friendship in practical terms and distinguish between being friends and merely acquaintances.

We will begin by identifying different types of friendships, and how these friendships typically develop. How do we move from simply *being friendly* to actually becoming friends? We uncover the power of choosing a loving attitude toward those of a different race. How do we handle misunderstandings and hurt feelings? How and what can we learn from our cultural differences? How do friendships enrich the lives of both individuals? These are the questions we seek to answer with real-life illustrations.

We believe that if every Christian had at least one friend of a different culture or race, it would radically change race relations in our country. Many are asking, "What can I do? I am only one person." An ancient Chinese proverb says, "The journey of a thousand miles begins with one step." We believe that building cross-cultural friendships is that first step. We encourage you to join us in promoting such friendships by putting into practice the biblical principles you'll discover in *Life-Changing Cross-Cultural Friendships*.

CHAPTER 1

An Unexpected Friendship

(Clarence) In 1968, my best friend was Russell. I was fourteen. He was a year younger than me. He attended an integrated school that was predominantly Caucasian. Many of us in the Black community called it a White school.

I attended a school with all-Black administration, faculty, and students, no diversity at all. I attended this school because Jean, my older sister, was a brilliant student and the best academic Black students were sent to this school because of its accelerated scholastic emphasis and opportunities.

Russell and I lived about a five-minute bike ride from each other in our all-Black neighborhood. In our minds, our neighborhood was cool! There were college professors, businessmen and women, public-school teachers, preachers, plus all-city and all-state athletes. I knew of only one single-parent mom in this vast Black community. Amazingly, everyone knew each other.

Any adult could correct a child they saw misbehaving. Once, a woman in my community saw me being mischievous. She asked, "Who are your parents?" Armed with this information, she took me home, where she explained my actions to my mom in excruciating detail. Once this lady left, Mom said, "How could you embarrass me in front of my new friend?" My foolish reply: "Mom, you just met her, and you didn't see what she said I did." Mom wasn't happy with my response, which was followed by a spanking. Actually, in my neighborhood, we didn't call it a spanking. We called it a "whooping." Though I hated getting whoopings, they probably saved my life! Several of my childhood friends agree with me.

So that was the culture that Russell and I experienced as two Black junior high school students back in 1968 in Winston-Salem, North Carolina.

(Gary) In 1968, my wife and I, with our four-year-old daughter, had recently moved to Winston-Salem. While school integration had started a decade earlier, most Black students continued to attend all-Black schools, and White students continued to attend all-White schools. Then in 1971, the United States Supreme Court mandated integrated schools.

I was beginning my career as an associate pastor of a church, working primarily with junior high and high school students. The population of the city was pretty evenly divided: fifty-fifty, White and Black. Racial tensions were running high. I remember waking up one morning and finding the National Guard stationed on the streets outside our apartment.

I had grown up in a Christian home and had been taught

that all humans are made in the image of God and should be respected. At the same time, we simply accepted racial segregation as a cultural norm. As a young pastor, I certainly did not know what I could do to improve racial tensions. I was about to find out.

An Unexpected Invitation

(Clarence) Russell was a ladies' man. Most girls said he was cute. I thought these girls had poor eyesight, but the girls themselves were certainly cute.

Some White girls who attended school with Russell invited him to their church, which had a new gym. In North Carolina, we valued basketball, tobacco, and Baptists—in that order. Basketball was my god at that time. So once Russell invited me to go with him to this new gym, I was all in. Basketball, plus girls—have mercy!

In the Black community, there was an unwritten rule that you never went to a White function by yourself because you might not return alive. Russell was really short. He was only four foot seven. I was much taller, standing at four foot eight. So I would be his bodyguard.

There was only one small problem. Blacks and Whites didn't socially interact much in Winston-Salem. Four years earlier, on July 2, 1964, the Civil Rights Act was signed into law, but not much had changed. Dad couldn't get a promotion beyond being a janitor. We continued to be called niggers frequently, or many Whites would give us what we called their look of disdain. The Ku Klux Klan had parades downtown, at least until the Black Panthers showed up. By and large, society was still segregated, especially the churches and schools.

An Unexpected Response to This Invitation

Can you imagine how my parents felt when I asked them if I could go to a White church to play basketball, if only to protect Russell? Unbeknownst to me, this was a serious issue. Some of my relatives viewed it as possibly a life-threating situation. Remember, this was 1968. There were race protests, and Black-church bombings and lynchings were frequent occurrences.

My parents had all of my relatives over to our house to determine whether I could go to a White church to play basketball. This meeting created an opportunity for me to meet some of my relatives for the first time. Still, I couldn't comprehend the gravity of my request. Dad, as a boy in South Carolina, saw one of his friends looking at a White girl. Dad's friend was lynched later that day. No way were Russell and I going to tell them that this invitation came from White girls!

This family town-hall meeting lasted for a few hours. The consensus was that Russell and I couldn't go. My family, like most Black families in the 1960s, went to church. The Black church was not and is not just about religion. It had and still has a tremendous social influence too. It was and continues to be an escape from the White world, if only for a few hours. I was not a Christian. I didn't care for church, because by the time we got home every Sunday, the pro football game on TV was almost always over. But as Mom was about to end the meeting, I blurted out in desperation, "Jesus will be with us!" I certainly didn't know Jesus personally, even though I'd been baptized when I was nine years old and sang in our youth choir. But that phrase changed Mom's attitude. She influenced everyone else and we got my family's permission to go to this White church.

After securing our permission, I was given two talks. One was not to flirt with or touch a White girl, because that could lead to being lynched. The other was the Talk regarding White people and the police. "They are very dangerous, even if they seem to like you. Be polite. Say, 'Yes, sir' or 'Yes, madam.' Don't question them. Don't ask for anything. Don't expect equal treatment. Don't change your facial expression if they call you a negative term. Don't tell them where you live. Don't be disrespectful in any way. Do whatever it takes to get back home, because we love you."

Initial Steps to Crossing Cultural Barriers

Russell and I walked to this church gym. It was a little more than four miles from our homes. Less than a mile from the church, we crossed railroad tracks. Often in American cities, many culturally or racially different communities were separated by railroad tracks. Almost immediately after we crossed these railroad tracks, White people driving by greeted us with just about every racial slur you could imagine. They threw empty Coke and beer bottles at us.

Finally, we saw the church. Just before we crossed the

street, some White guy jumped out of the bushes. He asked us, "Are you saved?" I responded, "Saved from what?" He told us that we needed Jesus Christ in our lives (which was true). He demanded that we pray right then and there to ask Jesus to forgive us for our sins and to come into our hearts. We refused. He told us that we were going to hell and walked away upset. This guy never asked our names or introduced himself to us. He never asked how we were doing. I said to Russell, "These girls better be really pretty, because of all of the stuff we have had to deal with just to get there."

Finally, we entered the gym. It was a brand new gym. The basketball floor looked so inviting. We were the only two Blacks out of what seemed like at least one hundred White kids. I felt like we'd have to fight our way out of there once Russell was done talking to his girls.

(Gary) I immediately saw Russell and Clarence enter our church gym. How could I miss them—two young Black men in a sea of White faces? I was encouraged to see some of our students greet them and engage them in conversation. Other students seemed not to even notice them, because they continued talking with their friends or playing games. I glanced around the room to see the reaction of the adults who were present to help with the activities of the evening. One of them pointed to the two young men as if I had not seen them. I nodded my head and raised my hands as if to say, "Relax, everything is fine."

I did not immediately walk to meet them. I did not want to intimidate them. I was glad to see them laughing with the students with whom they were talking. Eventually, students started moving to different game sites and the leader of the basketball game yelled, "Who wants to play basketball?" I noticed the two young men responding to the call. So I moved in their direction, introduced myself, asked their names, and welcomed them to our youth night. Little did I know that was the beginning of a lifelong relationship with Clarence.

(Clarence) The White kids didn't seem to care that we were there. Some were pretty friendly. Some of the adults gave us the look of disdain that I was used to seeing from Whites. But some of the adults seemed genuinely glad to see us.

I went to the basketball court because that was where I was the most comfortable and I felt I could win. There was volleyball, ping-pong, and other games. It wasn't long until a slender, tall White man with glasses came onto the basketball court. He introduced himself. His name was Gary Chapman. He was really nice.

After we played for some time, everyone was called together for a short Bible study. Gary taught the Bible study. He asked questions instead of lecturing. He seemed to really be interested in our answers. After the study, we played some more. Then everyone stopped and the adults fed us. Then Gary told us how we could become Christians. Even though I was in church every Sunday, I couldn't remember hearing how I could have a personal relationship with Jesus Christ. That was new and interesting.

(Gary) I always sought to keep the Bible study brief but meaningful. I found that students are willing to talk if someone is willing to ask questions and listen to them. I also found that when I expressed interest in their thoughts and ideas, some students would linger after the study to ask me questions. I felt that these informal conversations gave them a chance to share their struggles in a safe setting. After the meal, I always shared a brief word about what it means to be a Christian and told them that I would be happy to talk with anyone who wanted to talk about their relationship with God. In this informal setting, many young students committed their lives to Christ. Nothing brings me greater satisfaction than seeing young people begin their personal journey with Christ.

As I remember, I saw Russell and Clarence getting ready to leave, and I said, "So good to have you guys here tonight. I hope you had a good time and will come back. We are here the same night every week, and you are always welcome."

(Clarence) An older girl (sixteen or seventeen years old), Sara, who had a car, heard that Russell and I were walking home. She and her older brother, Gene, offered to drive us home. We accepted because we knew we'd be safe from bottles if we were with them.

The next week, Sara and Gene picked us up from my house. Sara drove. Having a White girl pick us up and drive us generated conversations with my male peer neighbors, who were trying to figure out how I was getting a White girl to come pick me up. They were a little jealous. They would ask me, "How are White girls different from Black girls?" This increased my coolness with the guys. The other parents were concerned about my safety and the wisdom of my going to the White side of town, even if it was a church. Russell and I did have some fear for our safety, but at thirteen and fourteen years old, we were willing to risk our safety for the excitement of this forbidden world of integration. We continued to attend this weekly event for the next two years.

Unexpectedly Reexamining
My Worldview

(Gary) Having Russell and Clarence come to our church gym for two years, and seeing the way our students welcomed and engaged them, was so encouraging. I knew in my heart that they were stepping out of their comfort zones when they first came, but I could see that they were feeling loved and accepted. With racial tension in the city and across the country, I felt I was seeing a picture of what things should be like.

(Clarence) Ever since I could remember, I heard, not from my parents but from my community, "Never trust White people. And if you are going to be successful, you'll have to be twice or three times as good." It was ingrained in me.

As I mentioned earlier, my mother worked for a sales organization that involved giving home demonstrations of her product. Her branch managers were Charlie and Peaches (not their real names), a White couple. They were so kind! I was shocked, because they were White. Their teenage daughter often picked me up and put me on her horse with her. Then she would ride me around their property. I was probably about six years old.

Charlie, Peaches, their daughter, and the White people who worked for them were extremely kind to my dad, mother, sister, and me. They treated us as equals. They wouldn't eat at places that would not serve my family and other Blacks when we were on vacation trips together up and down the East Coast. My mother won these trips by achieving or exceeding sales goals.

Therefore, I could no longer say that all Whites were

17

bad. But I didn't think of them as White. At six years old, my eyes could see our differences, but my mind could not process them.

It was eight years later before I met another White person who was genuinely kind to me. This was Gary, the White man who played basketball with us at this White church gym. Again, I saw he was White, but didn't think of him as White. After two years of watching Gary Chapman, I realized that he had something in his life that I didn't. It was a personal relationship with Jesus Christ. I knew I needed Jesus, but I didn't want a White man to introduce me to Christ.

Then the White girls whom we met at the church youth night invited us to go on a retreat with them. It was a great deal—girls, three meals daily, horseback riding, fishing, away from home for two and a half days! I'm sure my parents appreciated having this break from me.

An Unexpected Life Change

(Gary) When I heard that Clarence and Russell had signed up to go on the retreat with our youth group, I was both pleased and a little apprehensive. What would the White parents think or say when they heard that we were having two Black young men going on a weekend retreat with us? These were days of great racial tension. Both Whites and Blacks had distrust for each other. And the White parents did not have the advantage of knowing Clarence and Russell. These parents had not attended our gym youth nights. All they would know is that two Black guys were going to be with our youth group on a retreat. It seems to me that assuming the worst of someone based on skin color is a form of racism. I prayed that God would not let this become divisive.

The word did get out, and I had a few phone calls from concerned parents. But when I explained that we knew Russell and Clarence, that they had been a part of our youth group for two years, that our youth saw them as friends, and that I fully trusted them, parents agreed to let their teens go on the retreat.

Sadly, such mistrust between Whites and Blacks still exists in many places, which unfortunately includes people of faith. It is only as we get to know each other that walls are torn down. We say we believe that all men are created equal, but until we get to know each other, we are not likely to treat each other as equals. I was grateful that the retreat went forward and God continued his work in the hearts of students and parents.

(Clarence) The retreat was life changing for me. It was a Saturday, May 9, 1970, in Hillsville, Virginia. After dinner, we had the evening gathering. Gary preached. During his sermon, he asked, "Is your life complete, or is something missing in your life?"

I had great parents and a wonderful sister who loved me. I made the high school basketball team (one of the best in the state). I was a B student. I was in the cool group in school. And even though we were poor, I lived in a great neighborhood. Yet I struggled with racism, being short, loneliness, insecurity, and emptiness, and sometimes I thought about suicide.

Gary said, "If something is missing in your life, stay at your table and someone will talk with you. If you are fine, you are dismissed."

Russell and I were the only ones who stayed behind. Russell was not emotional about asking Christ into his life. But I was very emotional and fought back tears.

Sam, a member of a university track team, was sitting with me. He was my cabin counselor. He began talking with me about accepting Christ, and Gary joined him. Gary quoted John 3:16, but not in a way that I had ever heard before. He said, "For God so loved Clarence, that he gave his one and only Son, that if Clarence believes in him, Clarence shall not perish but have eternal life." Even though I wasn't a Christian, I knew that wasn't correct. So I told Gary, "That verse doesn't go like that."

Gary said, "Clarence, when God is talking about the world, he is talking about you. God can love all of us at the same time." I never thought about Jesus Christ personally loving me. It blew me away! That night I asked Jesus Christ to forgive me of my sins, to come into my life, and to make me the person he wanted me to be. From that moment, my whole life was changed. I was on a different course. I knew that I was an authentic Christian.

The retreat was in the mountains, and it was cold. I had never been camping, and I did not have a sleeping bag. I didn't know to bring blankets. The first night, I borrowed a blanket but felt like I almost froze to death. The second night, after accepting Jesus Christ into my heart, I was still probably physically cold. But I didn't feel cold. There was a warmth inside that I had never experienced before.

As soon as I returned home, I told Dad and Mom and Jean, my sister, that they all needed to be saved. They looked at me like I was crazy, because we went to church every Sunday. I certainly did not approach it in a very good way, but I wanted them to experience what I had experienced.

My profanity began to decrease, as did some of my other bad actions. I used to be one way with church people and another with my friends. Now my life continued to drastically change.

(Gary) There is no greater joy for a Christian than to see someone accept the love and forgiveness of God. I was thrilled to see Clarence genuinely commit his life to Christ. I knew in my heart that God had great plans for him in the future.

I was also grateful that I did not hear negative reports from parents after the retreat. I asked the students to let their parents know that Clarence accepted Christ. I think they were glad to hear this and would have felt guilty if they complained.

I did not know that we were going to become lifelong friends.

Your Thoughts

1. Do you have a friend or friends of a different culture or race? If so, how did you meet?
2. If you don't have a friend of a different culture or race, why do you think this is so?
3. Would you like to have a friend of a different culture or race? Why or why not?
4. If you do have a friend or friends of a different culture or race, how did you feel during your initial encounter? Why?

5. What was it about this other person that drew you to him or her?

6. What do others in your community say about having friends of a different culture or race? How does what they say influence you?

7. Whether or not you have friends of a different race or culture, what do you think some of the benefits would be of having a friend who is different from you? Why?

8. What do you think is God's perspective about his children having friends who are different from them?

CHAPTER 2

Different Levels of Friendship

Russell and I had just crossed Coliseum Drive. It was the north Black-White boundary of our segregated community. Once we crossed this east- and westbound major road with four lanes, we were now in the White community. But this area was safe because Blacks frequently shopped at the stores in the strip mall and went to the Coliseum, where the Wake Forest University basketball team played its home games. The Coliseum was located to the east of us on the other side of the Cherry-Marshall expressway, which went north and south through town.

On our way home from a fast-food restaurant, Russell and I saw Phil, a White guy about our age, playing football in the grass in front of his apartment complex. Phil invited us to play. Russell and I quickly dropped our bags of food on the ground and played football. We were surprised that White guys would ask us to play. We had so much fun and the color of our skin made no difference to them.

Phil was especially funny. Whenever he received a hard tackle, he would turn red and always say a particular curse word, drawing out the syllables. It sounded so funny that we all laughed.

I've never forgotten Phil, I guess because he was one of the first White guys my age who treated me as an equal and with respect.

We never met his parents. Our friendship didn't last more than a month or so. I don't know whether he moved or his parents made him stop playing with us. I like to think he moved into a house, since he was living in an apartment.

We never talked about anything. We just played football.

Some Benefits of Friendship

What comes to your mind when you think of the word *friendship?* Is it someone who is always there for you? Or someone you have known all your life? Or someone with whom you enjoy spending time? Someone with whom you can be open and honest and know they will not reject you? Ask a dozen people this question and you will likely get a dozen answers. What most people will agree on is that there are different levels or types of friendships.

Humans are social by nature. God designed us to be relational creatures. We want to relate to others. We want to love and be loved. We want people with whom we can share life. Life's deepest meaning is found in relationships—first of all with God, and then with fellow humans. If we don't feel socially and emotionally connected to others, it adversely affects our mental health. In contemporary culture, loneliness has become a major problem. The sense that no one knows me, sees me, or cares about me can lead from loneliness to depression. So developing friendships greatly enhances our well-being. And developing friendships across racial and cultural lines not only leads to deeper understanding but also can enhance spiritual and emotional health.

Before we discuss how to develop friendships, it's helpful to consider a variety of what we call prefriendship encounters.

Invisible Encounters

As we described in the introduction, interracial contact is inevitable in America. It would be almost impossible for most people not to encounter people of a different race—in a grocery store or any other business open to the public, at sporting events, in most vocational settings. In many of these encounters, we don't make eye contact or in any way acknowledge the other person's presence. In a huge city, one may pass thousands of people simply walking down the street. Time would not permit our acknowledging every person whom we encounter. At a crowded sports event, the same would be true. In such encounters we know that we are in the presence of other humans, but we don't see them. They are invisible and we have no desire or make no attempt to make a personal connection. We are simply humans on the way to somewhere. No relationship is likely to develop from such invisible encounters.

Courteous Encounters

Courteous encounters are brief acknowledgments of those of a different race. If we are on the street, especially in small towns or rural areas, we look at the other person and nod and smile, perhaps with a soft "hi." We don't know their names and have no desire to learn them. We simply acknowledge them as fellow humans. We treat them with courtesy, being friendly minded.

Socially Expected Encounters

Socially expected encounters occur most often in the halls of our places of employment. As we near the other person, we say, "Good morning." We may even add, "How are you today?" The expected response is, "Fine. How are you?" We respond, "Fine, thank you." We may know their name, and if so we add it to our "good morning." We may see this person daily or several times a week, but we know almost nothing about them and make no effort to get to know them. We are simply doing the polite thing in our culture.

None of these encounters are likely to lead to a friendship. They are simply humane ways of responding to fellow humans. There is nothing wrong with these responses. They are far better than giving looks of disdain or saying derogatory words as you encounter someone of a different race or culture. They are simply socially acceptable ways of responding.

On the Road to Friendships

The first step after a prefriendship encounter is getting acquainted. Many of us have acquaintances of a different race or culture. These relationships may develop between work associates, classmates at school, or people in other social settings. We know each other's names. We sit in some of the same meetings. We may even have lunch together. We talk business or sports. But our conversations rarely get personal. If someone asks us if we are friends, we would likely say, "Yes, we work together." But our relationship is limited to work, school, church, or some other social setting, If one of us leaves the company or goes to a different school or church, we likely would no longer have any contact with each other.

(Clarence) My mom often said, "An acquaintance is someone who may like you but when difficult times come, tends to leave when the good times do." An acquaintance is not a person who is committed to you or to being in a relationship with you, unless it is beneficial to them. You may treat each other with dignity and respect, and thus have a cordial relationship, but are you really friends?

But becoming acquainted with someone and relating in a friendly manner is a necessary step in building a friendship. Many people are acquainted with someone of a different race or culture, but often that is as far as it goes. We believe that many of these relationships could become genuine and beneficial friendships.

Let's consider a variety of types or levels of friendship.

Situational Friendships

One of the first levels of friendship is what we are calling situational friendships. We share at a personal level, but our relationship is limited to a certain segment of our lives. We find ourselves brought together by work, sports, church, or some other common interest. We become acquainted and our conversations go beyond surface talk. We freely share our thoughts, feelings, opinions, and aspirations and encourage each other. We talk about our families and share our struggles and concerns. We really are friends, but our friendship is limited to our situation and continues only as long as we are in that situation. We never relate to each other outside that context. If one of us drops out of our golf foursome or loses a job, the friendship dissolves.

(Clarence) Often I have been the first African American to work for a predominately White Christian nonprofit or for a predominately White church. Initially, because it was such an enormous transition for me, I assumed that the White Christians with whom I worked felt the same way I did about friendship. During these friendships at various ministries, we discussed virtually everything and even prayed together. I thought we bonded and that our friendship went beyond work.

The first time I left a predominately White Christian organization, I was surprised and hurt that the White Christians who I thought were my friends really weren't. Were they racists? Maybe, but I believe that for them I was a workplace friend, not a personal friend. No matter what we discussed or the depth of the discussion, we never did anything with our families outside of work. After working in several predominately White organizations, I was no longer surprised when none of my White coworkers were invested enough in our relationship to maintain our workplace friendships.

One of my African American friends worked for a conservative Christian college for seven years in an extremely visible position. After he left that college, he was devastated because none of his White friends ever contacted him after he left the job.

In both of these illustrations, our friendships were genuine. My friend and I both felt accepted, loved, and encouraged by our coworkers. What we did not realize until later is that our friendship was a situational friendship for them.

(Gary) A friend of mine shared a similar experience. "I felt really close to my golf buddies. We played every week for years. We talked freely about our families and everything. We disagreed about political issues, but it did not dampen our friendship. But when I had to drop out to care for my wife when she had a life-threatening disease, only two of the guys called me once within the first month. After that, I never heard from any of them." He was describing a situational friendship.

Situational friendships are good while they last. We have no desire to discredit them. They make for a better work environment or whatever common interest brought us together. This type of friendship is common. But if we don't understand that what seems like a personal friendship might well be a situational friendship, we can be deeply hurt when the situation changes.

Of course, if we are the one who is hurt when our friends don't reach out after we leave the situation, we could consider reaching out to them. Typically, we don't do this. Why? Because we are all egocentric—self-centered. We reason, "If they don't care enough to reach out to me, then I won't reach out to them." Or it might be a cultural difference and we realize that we really don't understand the other culture. This may lead to a reluctance to reach out because of fear of further rejection. So the friendship dies a natural death. But if we did make a call and invited them to lunch, assuming we still live in the same town, we may find that they are open to a personal friendship. Or we may find that they are truly not interested in keeping the relationship alive. Either way, because we took the initiative to reach out, we will likely process our emotions in a healthy manner.

Professional Friendships

Professional friendships are sometimes established between people who are in the same profession. For example, a White pastor shared that he was friends with some Black pastors in his city. They met at an annual prayer retreat for pastors. Part of the retreat involved pastors from different cultures getting into small groups, sharing their stories, and then praying for each other. After the retreat, this pastor called some of the Black pastors to follow up on the things that were shared at the retreat. Later, some of these pastors initiated calls to him. So they developed a relationship on the phone.

Then they began to have lunch together from time to time. They shared information about their families and prayed for each other's children. They also shared about their ministry challenges and successes. They developed a true friendship in which they trusted each other and knew that they genuinely cared for each other and would help each other in any way possible. Two of these pastors began to share pulpits once a year. Each pastor would bring the choir from his church and lead the congregation in worship. When either pastor was struggling with a problem, they felt free to call each other for prayer and advice.

When in 2020 the covid pandemic was followed by more racial tension in America, the White pastor felt free to call his ministry friends and get their perspective and advice. He said, "Because we are friends, I knew they would share openly with me. If we had not been friends, I would have been reluctant to call a Black pastor whom I did not know. I deeply appreciate my friendship with these pastors. They have greatly enriched my life."

Such professional friendships often develop between business leaders who work in the same type of business. I know funeral directors who have developed friendships with other funeral directors. They sometimes share vehicles and come to each other's aid when needed. Business leaders often meet at professional conferences or retreats and from there develop friendships. But it is not that often that these friendships cross racial or cultural lines.

American secular professional leaders know that they can't compete for global dollars if their companies aren't diverse. These professional leaders have also learned that a cross-cultural workforce increases its sales market, problem-solving ability, productivity, retention of people of color and women, and innovation—all resulting in profit.

Professional leaders who are driven by a desire for excellence want their companies and organizations to be the best in their field, with unparalleled success that increases annually. Who doesn't want that for their organization?

We believe that if professional leaders were intentional about building mutually beneficial cross-cultural professional friendships, they would be laying a foundation for greater success for themselves and their organizations. Their organizations would model cross-cultural leadership in their community by positively impacting race relations, and would be personally more ready to lead in a diverse world.

Mentoring Friendships

Another type of friendship is a mentoring friendship. The word *mentor* means "an experienced and trusted advisor." Our first mentors are typically our parents. When we were children, they were certainly more experienced than we. Most parents can also be trusted to advise their children wisely. As we get older, God often brings into our lives other experienced and trusted advisors. Many of us have had such advisors in our lives. We might not have called them mentors, but they took time to get to know us and to share their wisdom with us. They were truly our friends. Mentors may be short-term or long-term friends, but they greatly impact our lives.

(Clarence) One of my mentors was the late Dr. T. B. Maston, former professor of ethics at the seminary which I attended. He taught me how White systems work and why. He taught me about power brokers. And he explained to me why his peers of color preferred the term *Negro*. I did not like this term because for my peers and me, it had the connotation of slavery. But Dr. Maston said, "My peers of color embraced the term *Negro*." I was fascinated to hear that.

Other mentors are Dr. William Pannell, an African American, an author, and a former seminary professor, and

Gordon Loux, who is Caucasian and a former executive for several Christian organizations and a college. Dr. Pannell is now in his nineties. When he calls me, it is such a special time for me. He lovingly encourages and challenges me. Several years ago, Gordon began mentoring me as I developed my nonprofit. He is full of wisdom and encouragement. Both of these men made a significant investment in my life. What was and is encouraging to me is that we could strongly disagree, but it never affected our relationship. I think our disagreements made us closer because we so respected each other. Therefore, we respected each other's ideas.

Another mentor, who was more of a father figure to me, was the late Bob Cook. I was drawn to Bob because of the way he prayed. Also, not only were his adult children Christ followers, so were his grandchildren. I thought, "This man is doing something right!" He taught me so much about Jesus and how to love a wife and children. He and his family modeled legacy to me and my family. Bob and I usually met once a week. It was a precious and impactful time. He was so easy to access; I knew I could call him at any time.

Then there is Gary Chapman, whom I affectionately call Dad from time to time. I love it when he signs his emails "Dad." He has always been there for me. More than anyone, Gary has seen the good, the bad, and the ugly in my life. And he never walked away from me. He has given so much to my late mom, my sister, my wife, my girls, me, and our ministry. Gary has been involved in every major decision that I have made.

Because of Bob Cook and Gary Chapman, I have four spiritual sons whom I mentor. Bob and Gary exposed me to the biblical concept of investing in people and spiritual reproduction. For this I am deeply grateful.

(Gary) What Clarence did not say is that mentoring is a two-way process. Yes, the mentor is usually older and with more experience, but he or she also learns from the friendship. In our friendship, I have learned much from Clarence. His courage as a junior high student to attend an all-White youth group spoke volumes to me. His consistency in studying the Bible with me in his high school years communicated his eagerness to learn and to grow in his relationship with Christ. His educational journey through college and seminary spoke of his dedication to following God's plan for his life. I can identify with the apostle John, who said, "I have no greater joy than to hear that my children are walking in the truth" (3 John 4). His life and ministry have been a great encouragement to me.

I was introduced to the mentoring concept by Jim Murk, who was my mentor when I was a college student. Jim took me into his family and met with me weekly to study and discuss how the Bible applies to daily life. I knew then that I wanted to do for others what Jim did for me.

Cross-Cultural Mentoring

Any effective mentoring relationship should be mutually beneficial for the mentor and the mentee because they learn from each other.

When Gary began discipling me, it was risky for both of us. I knew it was dangerous for me to walk to his house even during the daytime after I crossed the railroad tracks. I felt it could be difficult for him because of the way one neighbor looked at him. He and his family could be ostracized or worse.

Cross-cultural mentoring may lead both the mentor and mentee where neither has been before because of their culturally different backgrounds. Both need to have open minds because they most likely view life through different filters.

The mentor may feel nervous or even unqualified because he or she is from a different culture. The mentee may be worried about what those of his or her race may think if a person of another culture or race is his or her mentor. And there's the question of credibility: Is this truth really true? Or does it have cultural or racial influence?

There has to be a trust factor. Whatever drew you to this mentor is key. Let cultural or racial differences be an asset and not a detriment. Patience and faith in God make all the difference in the relationship. Don't avoid conflict. Avoiding conflict will hinder a God-given opportunity to develop genuine intimacy.

A cross-cultural mentor-mentee relationship provides both participants a more accurate worldview. And the relationship helps both to be more sensitive to people of other cultures.

Don't let fear keep you from experiencing a life-changing opportunity.

Close Personal Friendships

Close personal friendships are not based on the situation, nor are they necessarily mentoring relationships. They may have started as situational or mentoring friendships, but they grow much deeper. This kind of friendship is between two people who, to use a biblical picture, feel closer than brothers or sisters. Their hearts are knit together in a deep commitment to each other. They genuinely seek each other's well-being. These are the kind of friendships that greatly impact each other for good. Once established, they tend to last for a lifetime.

(Clarence) When I was helping the youth pastor of a White megachurch, one of the young White men, David, asked me if I would be his friend. I was his camp counselor at the church's summer camp. He and other White guys would come to my house. Mom would offer them something to eat, but only David would eat whatever my mom cooked.

We became extremely close. How did we get so close? First, David asked me to be his friend for his senior year in high school. This was 1979 and there was still a lot of racial tension in our town. David's asking for my friendship was risky for him. He could have lost his friends and experienced physical violence. There was a spirit about David that simply said I could trust him, the same way dogs can sense whether a human likes them or is afraid of them. (I believe most people of color can sense how a White person feels about them by the spirit, actions, and words of that particular person.)

Another reason David and I became close was his acceptance of Mom's cooking, even when his peers did not. David demonstrated respect and equality in his response to my mom's hospitality. Hospitality is critical in relationships with most people of color. After David's acceptance of Mom's hospitality, I knew that I could take him into a Black setting and he would be cool.

David was never ashamed or embarrassed to be with me. Neither was I his token Black friend to show off.

We were transparent and honest in our relationship. He was eighteen years old and I was twenty-six. I don't think David was looking for a Black friend. I think he was looking for an older brother, because his was off in college. We never avoided talking about race, but it was never a primary issue for us.

Respect was another crucial foundation for our closeness.

We had things in common. We both loved having fun. His mother would frequently send us to the grocery store. At the checkout counter, David would often say, "What else did Mom say we should get? We'll have to make an executive decision." He loved looking at the shocked faces surrounding us.

His parents' accepting me was also a factor in our developing a closeness. His parents trusted me. Whenever they went out of town, they asked me to stay with their son, because he was still in high school. They invited my family over to their home for dinner. Mom and Dad never invited them to our house for dinner. Mom was ashamed because we lived in a "shotgun" house. A shotgun house is a linear house that theoretically, a bullet shot from the front door could go through to the back door without hitting anything. The word *shotgun* originates from the Yoruba word *togun*, which means "house" or "gathering place."

David and I talked about everything and enjoyed doing things together. He taught me how to drive a manual gearshift in his Triumph Spitfire on the Blue Ridge Parkway. It was sweet. We remained close friends until his tragic death in a car crash. I was in seminary when this happened. His parents asked me to speak at his memorial service. Emotionally it was hard to speak, but I wanted to honor him and our friendship. Had he not been killed, we would still be close friends. We had a friendship that would have lasted a lifetime. I am glad we will have a reunion in heaven.

(Gary) One Black lady shared with me that she developed a friendship with a White lady at work. "She would come down to my desk and we would just talk. The thing was we didn't look at race. We just saw each other as a person. It was never about race. She just happened to be White and I happened to be Black. We hung out at the clubs. We just got to know each other. I stayed at her house, and she stayed at my house. We were both single at the time. We went to each other's house for Thanksgiving. We went on vacation together.

"Later when we both got married, we didn't see each other as much, but we still talked every day at work. Then several years ago, I moved out of state for another job. By this time we both had kids. But we are still close. Sometimes she will call and say, 'I just wanted to say hello.' She will send me cards, and I will call or send an email. We keep in touch. We know that we will always be friends. She is like a sister to me." I asked, "How long have you been friends?" She thought a minute and said, "Thirty years."

Their friendship illustrates how a relationship can move from a situational friendship into a close personal friendship beyond the work environment. It is also an example of how friendships often begin at one stage of life but continue to deepen as we grow older. Our situation changes, but our friendship continues. Close personal friendships across racial lines flourish when we not only see each other's culture or race but also see each other as persons, understanding that a person's culture or race is included in who that person is. Again, we ask, what would happen in our country, or in any country, if every Christian had at least one close personal friend of another race or culture?

Your Thoughts

1. How have you observed different levels or types of friendships in the lives of people with whom you are acquainted?
2. Can you think of another level or type of friendship in addition to those we have shared?
3. How would you describe the difference between an acquaintance and a friend?
4. Do you have different levels of friendship? Write the names of those with whom you are friends and place them in one of the categories.
5. Do you have friendships that you would like to move to a deeper level?
6. Do you have anyone to whom you are a mentor—investing your life in their life?
7. Do you have a mentor—someone who is older than you and whom you trust—who is investing their life in yours?

8. If you answered no to questions 6 and 7, consider asking God to give you someone in whose life you can invest your life, and for someone who will invest their life in yours.

9. If you have any type of friendship with someone of a different culture, what do you think are the benefits to you and to them?

CHAPTER 3

Friendship Begins with Courtesy and Patience

(Gary) In those early years, I didn't decide that I would develop a friendship with Clarence. I simply treated him as though he were a friend. That is what the word *courtesy* means. The English word comes from two Greek words. One means "the mind" and the other "friend." So to be courteous is to be friendly minded—to treat others as you would treat a friend. To me, this is where friendships begin. An ancient Hebrew proverb says, "A man who has friends must himself be friendly" (Prov. 18:24 NKJV).

What would life be like if we treated everyone we encountered as we would treat a friend? Let's say that you drive your car into a parking lot. You see an empty space and head for it, but you see another car headed for the same space. What do you do? Most of us speed up to get the space. But what would you do if you knew that the other person was one of your friends? Likely you would slow down and give the space to them. Why not do that for a stranger?

By nature, all of us are self-centered. But love focuses on the well-being of others. Loving people are courteous people. When courtesy becomes a lifestyle, we open the door to the possibility of building friendships across racial and cultural lines. We are called to love others as God loves us (John 13:34–35). But this is not something we do simply by self-effort. The Scriptures say that the love of God is poured into our hearts by the Holy Spirit (Rom. 5:5). So if we see ourselves as channels of God's love to everyone we encounter, we will treat everyone as a friend. This is what I did when I met Clarence and Russell. I simply treated them with the same dignity and respect I showed to the White teens in our youth group. I was encouraged to see so many of our teens do the same.

Cross-cultural friendships develop as you spend time together. Treating each other with courtesy is the first step in the process. Where might this begin for you? Likely by simply acknowledging those of a different race whom you encounter in daily life. At work, the grocery store, the shopping center, or a sports event, we all see those of another culture or race. Many times we don't even look them in the face and give a smile or a welcoming hello. Perhaps the first step is to ask God to help you see them as persons for whom Christ died. After a few smiles and hellos, you might engage them in conversation.

One White lady said, "I kept seeing the same African American lady in the grocery store each week. I had politely nodded at her a few times with a smile. One day I said, 'I've seen you several times. This must be your shopping day. What is your name?' She said, 'My name is Agnes.' I said, 'My name is Mary. Is your family doing okay?' 'Everyone except my mother,' she replied. 'So what's wrong with your mother?' I inquired. She told me about her mother's illness, and then I said, 'I am going to pray for your mother this week. What is her name?' 'Selma,' she said. That was the beginning of our friendship.

> Ask God to help you see others as a person for whom Christ died.

"After a few more conversations at the grocery story, I asked if I could visit her mother, and she agreed. I took flowers, and after talking with her, I prayed for her. Later, Agnes told me that her mother was shocked that a White woman would come to visit her. After that, Agnes and I started meeting at a restaurant for lunch, and after several conversations, I invited her to my women's Bible study at my house. She came, and now all of our ladies love her. I call her sometimes and tell her things she can pray for me. Friendship is a two-way street, you know." I do know, and I think of how many friendships could develop if we simply took the first step.

In cross-cultural friendships, there will be conflicts and misunderstandings. Why? Because all of us are influenced by our personal history. This is when patience becomes extremely important. In my relationship with Clarence and James, another of his friends, we had a misunderstanding early on.

(Clarence) Gary began to pick up James, my new best friend, and me at my house to drive us to the church gym.

The first time Gary picked us up was quite memorable! James and I were getting out of our chairs on the front porch as we saw Gary's car arrive. Gary jumped out of his car, smiling, and said, "You boys ready to go?" James, who was about six foot two with his Afro, responded, "I ain't no boy!"

What is funny about this now is that at the time, James was fifteen years old and I was sixteen. Many people thought of us as boys according to our ages. But the name *boy* was often used as a derogatory term by Whites to demean adult Black men. James and I were radicals and refused to allow any White person to call us boy.

Gary said, "After the meeting, we need to talk." So after the fun and the Bible study, the three of us talked for a long time about the word *boy*. Gary said, "If you two had been White, I would have said the same thing." Then he graciously listened to our perspective. We both liked Gary. He was very nice to us. We knew that as an adult man, he chose to spend time with us. This uncomfortable conversation made us all closer to each other. It gave all three of us a new perspective. Conflict can make you closer if it is handled correctly. So making a new friend, especially one from a different culture or race, may require grace and patience to open the door to understanding.

(Gary) After three years working with the youth at the church where I met Clarence, I was approached by a church on the west side of town to join their staff and start a ministry to college students. After much prayer, I really felt that was God's next step for me. So, in moving, I lost contact with Clarence for a few months. Later, when we reconnected, I was saddened to hear what had happened to Clarence and James at my former church.

(Clarence) A new youth pastor replaced Gary. His first words were "Blacks and Whites shouldn't worship together." He looked directly at James and me as he spoke. This was devastating news for me because James was not a Christian at the time. I wanted him to come to know Christ like I had. James and I had also invited

> Conflict can make you closer if it is handled correctly.

some of our Black friends to come to the gym because I also wanted them to know Christ. We found out later that what stimulated the pastor's comment about Blacks and Whites not worshiping together was the fact that our friends had been touching the White girls inappropriately. The girls told the youth pastor, and that was his response. Had the girls or he told James and me, we would have stopped that problem immediately. The girls were sad that James and I could no longer come to the gym. They said that they wished they had come to us first.

This situation had racial overtones, but it was more of a behavior issue that could have easily been corrected. The racial overtone was that we received only one strike and no grace. James and I wondered whether if our friends had been White, we would have been kicked out or just given a warning. At the time, I was curious to know what motivated his words, but I was not comfortable with this new youth pastor's demeanor. So I didn't ask him. I didn't learn what really happened until later at school when the girls told us. We never went back to that church.

Even with such a bad experience, I had to have patience to see what God would do. I also needed patience not to blame all White people for what one White person did, a person who seemed insensitive to people who were different from him.

God's Sovereignty in the Midst of Disappointment

(Clarence) The next year, because of forced integration, I attended what was probably the most prestigious and wealthiest White high school in the city at that time. It was named for the most successful businessman in the city. The way integration was done in our city was that all the Black high schools were reduced to ninth- and tenth-grade schools. All the White high schools remained senior high schools with eleventh and twelfth grades. This prestigious and wealthy White high school became the closest high school to my house, only three or four miles away, which was within walking distance.

Integration meant that no longer would I go to school with my Black schoolmates, whom I'd known since the second grade. No longer would I have Black teachers, who loved me and demanded academic excellence from me. No longer would I have Black male teachers. No longer would I have the high school basketball coach who recruited me. He had planned to start me as his point guard my junior year. I trusted him like a father.

No longer would there be discipline in the classroom in which the students respected and never spoke disrespectfully to a teacher without painful consequences. We Blacks were shocked that White students spoke disrespectfully to White teachers with no consequences. For example, if a White teacher told a White student to stop talking or making noise at his or her desk, it wasn't uncommon for that student to say no or "I'll do what I want." The White teacher didn't say anything else about it. It was like the White students were in charge. The previous year at my all Black high school, a six-foot-two, two-hundred-pound football player spoke disrespectfully to our Black teacher. She immediately sent one of my classmates to get the football and basketball coaches, both of whom were big Black men. They came to the class and took this football player out of the room. Thirty minutes later this football player with tears in his eyes apologized to our teacher and to us. The basketball coach said to all of us, "Don't you ever disrespect someone who is trying to teach you something, especially a Black woman. Your parents trust us to teach you so you can have a better life than they have."

Education in the Black community was huge. Black parents saw education as a key for their children to secure a better quality of life than they had. So Black parents would often spank their children or practice some kind of discipline to motivate their children to academic success.

My academic, athletic, and social communities were simultaneously destroyed.

Black and White teachers actually teach differently, and Black and White students learn differently. What I'm about to share with you is research that makes data-based generalizations—meaning that the findings do not apply to every individual.

The research of Dr. Edwin Nichols in his landmark study "The Philosophical Aspects of Cultural Difference" reveals that in general, people of European descent learn by counting and measuring: parts to the whole. Their learning style is linear, similar to an assembly line: A then B then C then D. If you think in terms of quality management, then objectives and milestones, things you can count and measure, are priority.

Africans, African Americans, Hispanics/Latinos, and Arabs generally understand something immediately without the need for reasoning (similar to a woman's intuition or my knowing I could trust David). These cultures think holistically. Often, they see the big picture without going through a process. This results in these cultures' desire to cut to the chase.

While I was serving as the first and only African American on a megachurch staff that was predominantly White, our leadership often had us do exercises to determine which way to lead the church. I remember expressing that I could see where they were trying to go and that their process wasn't necessary. One of the female leaders said, "Clarence, we have to do this process to get to where you are." The Caucasians were compartmental in their thinking. I was holistic. Neither was wrong or right, just different.

First Nations people or Native Americans tend to know things by reflection and spiritual receptivity. They tend to see the whole in cyclical movements like the seasons of the year. Knowledge is acquired from spiritual teachings and passed down to each generation. Usually, there is no dichotomy between scientific and spiritual knowledge.

Asians, Asian Americans, and Polynesians process information differently from all the other groups. In general, most Asians see the big and small picture simultaneously.

Having used Dr. Nichols' principles (with his permission) in my diversity training for approximately twenty years with faith-based and secular organizations, it is amazing to see how accurate his principles are.

If teachers aren't aware of these general cultural learning styles, the students of a culture different from the teacher loses, and so do the other students in the room. I had to adjust to a teaching style for Whites. School went from fun and daily excitement to a boring system that tolerated Blacks but certainly did not celebrate us.

Black teachers didn't just impart information but were students of us as individuals. They learned our strengths and weaknesses and used this information to get the best out of us. My White teachers taught without having a relationship with us students.

A friend of mine, Dr. Jeff Shears, who attended an historically Black college, often says that the nurturing he received there encouraged him to pursue his PhD.

One day in my upper-level eleventh-grade English class, my White teacher, Mrs. Smith, bragged about my one-page paper on classicism. I felt that she cared, and my grades dramatically improved in her class. I didn't have the heart to tell her that I wrote it while watching the late-night *Johnny Carson Show*.

In my Spanish class, I was not doing well. My Spanish teacher, who was Latino, made me stay after school to study. This attention made me feel cared for, and my grades skyrocketed. I went on to learn French, Portuguese, and New Testament Greek.

It was at this White senior high school that I ran into Carol, one of the girls who invited Russell to the White church with a gym where I met Gary Chapman. Carol babysat for the Chapmans and reconnected me with Gary. Without forced integration, it's possible that I might have never seen Gary again!

(Gary) I was so glad to get reconnected to Clarence after being apart for nearly a year. By this time, we had started a Friday night gathering for college students at our house. We had one student from Egypt and a couple from Asia, but most were White. So again Clarence and friends who came with him were the only African Americans. Our entire format was Q&A. Students could ask questions on any topic. I was not the "answer man," but I led the discussion. I thought Clarence would enjoy this setting even though he was still in high school. So I invited him. He started attending regularly. I observed that he was deeply committed to Christ and eager to learn. So I asked if he would like to come to my house on Saturday mornings and we could have some time studying the Bible together. He accepted the invitation, and for some time, we met every Saturday morning. It was through our time together that our friendship grew. At this stage, our friendship was a mentoring friendship. I really sensed that God had great plans for Clarence, and I wanted to do all I could to encourage him.

(Clarence) Every Saturday morning, I walked approximately four miles to Gary's house. Once I crossed the railroad tracks, the name-calling and bottles came my way. I walked by myself, breaking the unwritten Black rule, in order to learn more about God. I was always relieved to arrive at Gary's home without an incident. And while walking home, I didn't feel safe until I crossed the railroad tracks back into my community. We studied on Gary's back screened-in porch. I met Karolyn, his wife; Shelley, his daughter; and Derek, his son. Shelley and Derek were both very young.

I'll never forget that first Saturday. His neighbor, a White lady, who was outside in her yard, gave Gary a glare that made me fear for his safety. She looked at me, then at him as if to say with her eyes, "What are you doing letting *him* into your house?" Gary either didn't see it or it did not bother him. He and I were breaking some critical cultural rules!

(Gary) I think my neighbor's response was more one of shock than of condemnation. After our first meeting, I explained to her that Clarence was a friend I had known for some time and that we were studying the Bible together. After that, she seemed to understand. As you pursue cross-cultural friendships, be prepared to have conversations with others of your own race, helping them understand what you're doing.

In addition to his coming to our Bible studies, I also encouraged Clarence to memorize key Scripture verses. I had found this practice to be extremely helpful in my own life. He was also expressing the idea that perhaps God wanted him to be a pastor. I knew that memorizing Scripture would serve him well in his efforts to help others.

(Clarence) Once, I memorized the entire book of James, just to please Gary. He never asked me to do this. My motive was wrong. I desperately wanted the approval of a man. My dad loved me but was always working two or three jobs to support us. I didn't know whether he approved of me. I watched my parents learn to trust Gary with James and me. I guess they thought, "If he is a pastor who works with college students, leading Bible studies, and memorizing Scripture, he couldn't be too bad." They were adjusting to this new world of integration as much as I was.

One Sunday evening, James and I, along with Mike, Tim, Joe, and Bill, White guys we met at the Friday night college gatherings, decided to go to Gary's new church on the west side of town. We walked in late, and the choir stopped singing. The pastor, the late Dr. Mark Corts, got up and said something like, "Everything is fine. Nothing is wrong here. We're glad to have you. Now let's continue our service." That put everyone at ease. I felt safe and comfortable. Some of my Black friends' parents had said that Whites would lynch Blacks in that part of town. Of course, James and I thought we were fast enough to escape anyone chasing us. Besides that, we were with our White friends, who had cars. So we felt safe.

Eventually, James and I began to attend this new White church every Sunday night. I'd go to my Black church on Sunday mornings. Making friends at the White church was not my priority, but hearing God's Word was. Dr. Corts was an excellent teacher. I was a follower of Christ and wanted to learn everything I could. But we did make friends; some became lifelong friends.

(Gary) I was pleased with the way most of our church family responded to James and Clarence. They were indeed friendly minded, treating them as they would anyone else. Only a few people asked me, "What are they trying to do, coming to our church?" I would respond, "They are trying to worship God and learn more about the Bible. I hope that is what all of us are trying to do." That seemed to satisfy them. As they got to know James and Clarence, they saw that what I said was true.

Breaking down walls of division is not easy, but I believe that building friendships tears down walls, one block at a time. The more we get to know those of a different race or culture, the more we understand each other and learn how to help each other. I can only imagine what would happen if every Christian in America had at least one friend of a different race or culture. I believe we would change the emotional climate of race in our country.

> Building friendships tears down walls one block at a time.

It all begins with an attitude of love expressed as courtesy, being friendly minded, treating everyone we encounter as though they were a friend. Courtesy, followed with patience as we take time to work through initial misunderstandings, are the first steps to genuine friendships.

Your Thoughts

1. Courtesy (being friendly minded) is often the first step in beginning a friendship with someone. How would you treat someone of a different culture or race if you treated them as though they were your friend?

2. When you reflect on your encounters with someone of a different race, in what ways did you express a friendly attitude? What might you have done differently?

3. How do you typically handle conflict with a family member or friend?

4. How do you think conflict with someone of a different culture or race should be handled? Why?

5. What would be the benefits of talking through an uncomfortable conversation with a new friend of a different culture or race?

6. What are some of the payoffs of having patience with a friend who is different from you?

7. How do you feel when people are patient with you, especially if you are new or different?

CHAPTER 4

Friends Love Each Other

(Gary) Love is the most important word in any language—and the most confusing word. I say that love is the most important word because Jesus once said, "I am giving you a new commandment: Love each other. Just as I have loved you, you should love each other. Your love for one another will prove to the world that you are my disciples" (John 13:34–35 NLT). Jesus gave the non-Christian world the right to judge whether we are his disciples by the way we love each other. That makes love extremely important. I say that love is the most confusing word because we use it in many different ways. We say, "I love hot dogs. I love pizza. I love my new car. I love the mountains. I love the beach. I love my dog. I love classical music. I love rock." Then in a romantic setting we say, "I love you." What is that supposed to mean?

In this chapter, we are not going to discuss the various

ways in which we use the word love. Rather, we are going to define love in a cross-cultural friendship. This kind of love begins with an attitude and then expresses itself in our behavior. By attitude, I mean our fixed way of thinking or our mindset. Love chooses to seek the best for a friend. "I want our friendship to enrich your life" is the attitude of love. The opposite of love is selfishness. "I am in this relationship to meet my needs" is the attitude of selfishness. "If you meet my needs, if you make me happy, then I will continue in our relationship. If not, I will move on." Friendships will not develop between two selfish people. In true friendships, the attitude of love is essential.

> Love in a cross-cultural friendship begins with an attitude and then expresses itself in behavior.

Jesus Modeled How to Love

When we examine Jesus' lifestyle, we see love demonstrated. Peter said about Jesus, "He went around doing good" (Acts 10:38). He healed the sick, gave sight to the blind, spent time with people from all levels of society. Ultimately, he gave his life, not only for those of his generation but for people of all cultures and all generations. His coming to earth was motivated by love. "For this is how God loved the world: He gave his one and only Son, so that everyone who believes in him will not perish but have eternal life" (John 3:16 NLT). Jesus himself said, "For even the Son of Man came not to be served but to serve others and to give his life as a ransom for many"

(Matt. 20:28 NLT). It is this kind of love that builds friendships and identifies us as his disciples.

The best description of love in the Bible is found in 1 Corinthians 13:4–7. "Love is patient and kind. Love is not jealous or boastful or proud or rude. It does not demand its own way. It is not irritable, and it keeps no record of being wronged. It does not rejoice about injustice but rejoices whenever the truth wins out. Love never gives up, never loses faith, is always hopeful, and endures through every circumstance" (NLT). This is the kind of love that enables us to build cross-cultural friendships.

God actually commands us to love each other as he loves us. Anything God commands, he will enable us to do. Perhaps you are thinking, "I just can't initiate or be involved in a cross-cultural friendship because my family has historically been the victim of racial injustice or my family has been involved in some capacity of promoting racial injustice." The reality is we cannot love as Jesus loved without his help. The apostle Paul reminds us that indeed we have his help. "For we know how dearly God loves us, because he has given us the Holy Spirit to fill our hearts with his love" (Rom. 5:5 NLT). So we are to be channels of expressing God's love to each other—not by self-effort but simply by opening our hearts to the Holy Spirit so he can fill them with his love.

Our Emotions Can Hinder Our Love Efforts

Often our emotions push us away from each other. Past experiences, cultural assumptions, and stories we have heard from others can stimulate negative emotions toward those of a different race. If we follow these emotions, we will not seek to build friendships with "those people." But we know that building friendships cross-culturally is God's desire for his children. So we acknowledge our emotions, but we do not allow them to control our behavior.

Here is the thought process that leads us to loving those who are different from us:

- I need to line up the way I'm thinking with the Word of God.
- I need to line up my actions with the Word of God.
- Then, in time, my emotions will change.

You may feel fear while pursuing a friendship with someone of another race. You may feel confusion about what is appropriate to say and do. You may even feel angry when you feel like you've been accused of being a racist. We do not choose our emotions. We do choose our attitudes and we do choose our actions. A loving attitude and loving actions stimulate loving emotions and lead to friendships.

Jesus' Love Equals Action

(Clarence) My favorite demonstration of this process of loving is seen when Jesus faced the reality of the cross.

They went to the olive grove called Gethsemane, and Jesus said, "Sit here while I go and pray." He took Peter, James, and John with him, and he became deeply troubled and distressed. He told them, "My soul is crushed with grief to the point of death. Stay here and keep watch with me."

He went on a little farther and fell to the ground. He prayed that, if it were possible, the awful hour awaiting him might pass him by. "Abba, Father," he cried out, "everything is possible for you. Please take this cup of suffering away from me. Yet I want your will to be done, not mine."

—Mark 14:32–36 NLT

Obviously, Jesus was struggling emotionally with what was about to happen. He did not seek to hide his emotions. He shared them openly with his Father. It is as though he was saying, "This is how I am feeling right now in the flesh, but what I really choose is your will." When developing cross-cultural friendships, possibly the most important principle is this: Jesus overrode his feelings in order to be obedient to his Father. He did exactly what he is asking us to do. While emotions are natural, legitimate, usually healthy, and often appropriate, the love Jesus Christ modeled is more of an action than a feeling. This is why Jesus said, "You have heard the law that says, 'Love your neighbor' and hate your enemy. But I say, love your enemies! Pray for those who persecute you! In that way, you will be acting as true children of your Father in heaven" (Matt. 5:43–45 NLT). He is commanding us to love *even* our enemies. In his power, we can love our enemies with our words and our actions, even though we do not like our enemies. When we choose an attitude of love toward those of a different race or culture, even when we have negative or mixed emotions, we are following Jesus' example. A loving attitude leads to loving behavior, which opens the door to the possibility of becoming friends.

> When we choose an attitude of love toward those of a different race or culture, even when we have negative or mixed emotions, we are following Jesus' example.

Another barrier to building cross-cultural friendships is our self-image. Some people have a low self-image. They see themselves as unworthy of a friendship or think that they have nothing to offer anyone, let alone a cross-cultural friendship. For the Christian who struggles with self-esteem, knowing how God views us is extremely encouraging. In Genesis 1 we read:

> Then God said, "Let us make human beings in our image, to be like us. They will reign over the fish in the sea, the birds in the sky, the livestock, all the wild animals on the earth, and the small animals that scurry along the ground."

> So God created human beings in his own image.
> In the image of God he created them;
> male and female he created them.

> Then God blessed them.
> —GENESIS 1:26–28 NLT

God Values Us and We
Should Value Others

In this passage, God says that he wanted us before we were even born! He gave us value because he gave us his DNA. We have a purpose and a godly destiny. Some theologians have said that every time God sees us, he says, "Wow!" because we resemble him. God sees himself in us. Since God made us in his image, we are extremely valuable to him. Therefore, we are challenged to believe God's view of us. Every human is of infinite value, and God has a place for each of us in his kingdom.

This is a critical element in developing cross-cultural friendships, because each of us brings our unique God-designed self to the table of friendship. This means that we enter a cross-cultural friendship expecting that we will learn from each other. We do not view ourselves as inferior or superior but as equals in God's sight. Yes, we are racially and culturally different, but love allows each of us to enrich the life of the other.

> Enter a cross-cultural friendship expecting to learn from each other.

What does this look like in the normal flow of life? Here are some real-life examples.

(Gary) An African American lady named Robin had her own business cleaning houses. One of the homes she cleaned was owned by a White lady named Mary, who tended to think of Robin as only a housecleaner. Robin knew that each year, as winter approached, Mary planted pansies in the two large pots on her front porch. So Robin asked her, "Are you going to plant pansies on the front porch again this year?" Mary replied, "Yes, if I can find them. They are hard to find this year." So Robin went shopping and found pansies and planted them in the two pots. Mary was shocked and offered to pay for them. Robin said, "No, I want to give them to you because I love working for you." Mary was never again able to think of Robin as simply her housecleaner. She began to see her as a friend. Such expressions of love often open doors to friendship.

Karolyn and I often eat at a restaurant owned by a lady from Albania. We have always treated her in a friendly manner, but we have never sought to develop a deep friendship. One year, on the Wednesday before Thanksgiving, we decided to go there for dinner. At the end of our meal, the waitress told us that our meal was a gift from the owner. We were shocked, and I sensed that she genuinely liked us. In all my years of eating in restaurants, I had never had a restaurant owner give me a free meal. When someone gives me a thoughtful gift, I naturally feel a stronger bond with them. I entered this new friendship knowing I would learn from my Albanian friend. I also set aside any negative or mixed emotions in favor of an attitude that follows Jesus' example.

Perhaps you have heard the saying, "Actions speak louder than words." Jesus demonstrated this truth just before his crucifixion. While having dinner with his disciples, he took a basin of water and a towel and washed his disciples' feet. Then he stood up and said, "Do you understand what I was doing? You call me 'Teacher' and 'Lord,' and you are right, because that's what I am. And since I, your Lord and Teacher, have washed your feet, you ought to wash each other's feet. I have given you an example to follow. Do as I have done to you" (John 13:12–15 NLT). Leaders serve others! Such acts of love are often steps toward developing cross-cultural friendships. In our culture, we are not likely to express love by washing feet, but we do express love when we mow the grass of a friend who is in the hospital or away on vacation. Or a friendship might begin when you say to an elderly neighbor, "I am going to the grocery store. Is there anything I can get for you?"

If you have a particular skill, let your friends know that you will be happy to help when needed. Some time ago, I was out of town speaking when I got a call from Karolyn telling me that the furnace was not working. I asked her to see if the pilot light was burning. Her response was, "No. It is dark in there." So I suggested that she call Larry, a friend of ours. I knew he would be happy to help. She called an hour later and said, "Larry came over and it is working fine now." Friends are eager to share their skills with those they love. Sharing your skills is one way to show love within a cross-cultural friendship.

A Life-Changing Cross-Cultural Experience

Andrea Shuler, daughter of Clarence and Brenda, shared the following from her life: "In my work as an educator, I have observed young children holding hands with each other without regard to race. I am always encouraged when I see adults reach across racial lines and greet each other with a handshake, a hug, or a high five. In church I always notice when people of different races sit close to each other and talk with each other before and after the worship service. Sometimes I also observe this on public transportation. This is always encouraging to me.

"I recently spent a weekend with a White family with whom I have developed a friendship. I did not experience a moment of boredom, nor did I have much time to myself because the children were so happy to have me, and I don't think the color of my skin crossed their minds. I say that because I have been around other children who have asked questions about my appearance. In this household, the children were more interested in what music I listen to, how I spend my time, what authors, sports teams, and players I like, and most important, what style of jokes I find humorous.

"At the end of my visit, when they drove me to the airport to get my return flight home, I expected to be dropped off at the curbside. On the contrary, the mom parked and they all came inside so they could take turns hugging me goodbye. It was so powerful for bystanders to watch this White family publicly showing affection to a Black woman. This was not the norm in that area of the state, but there they were, treating me as a blood relative. This anecdote would not be complete if I did not tell you how it filled my heart to look back, expecting to see the backs of their heads as they walked away, but to my surprise, they remained at the barrier watching me go through the security line. They shouted goodbyes and waved me down the ramp until I was no longer in sight. I wish everyone could experience the deep joy of having friends of another race."

Jesus Loved across Cultural Lines

(Clarence) As we noted in the beginning of this chapter, Jesus instructed us to love others as he has loved us. He said, "Your love for one another will prove to the world that you are my disciples" (John 13:35 NLT). If Christians of different races or cultures demonstrate love for each other, we just might convince the non-Christian world that we are truly followers of Jesus. What, then, does it look like to love others in a cross-cultural friendship as Jesus loved us?

Possibly the best illustration of demonstrating love across cultural lines is Jesus' cross-cultural encounter with the Samaritan woman in John 4:1–42. The Jews and Samaritans did not like each other and avoided each other as much as possible. Let's see what Jesus did.

> *Step 1:* Jesus breaks a Jewish traditional law by traveling into Samaria. (In Luke 9:51–56, Jesus tried to go through Samaria, but the Samaritans rejected him.)
>
> *Step 2:* Jesus goes to where the Samaritan woman lived, demonstrating that his message of eternal life is for people of all races and cultures.
>
> *Step 3:* Jesus meets the woman on her own turf (the well), where she is rejected by other women.
>
> *Step 4:* Jesus breaks another Jewish traditional law by speaking to a Samaritan woman, who was always seen as ceremonially unclean by Jews, meaning he defiles himself by speaking with her.
>
> *Step 5:* Jesus makes himself vulnerable to the Samaritan

woman by asking for a drink of water (giving her the freedom to reject him).

Step 6: Jesus demonstrates staying power when the woman initially rejects him, but he doesn't go away.[2]

The six steps that Jesus took to initiate a cross-cultural relationship with the Samaritan woman express the following characteristics of loving someone of a different culture:

- *Acceptance of or openness to those who are different from us.* Acceptance is what led Jesus to travel through Samaria, which was forbidden for Jews. Acceptance and openness today are demonstrated when a person of a minority culture enters a room in which he or she is the only minority, and a person of the majority culture approaches him or her with a welcome, and then takes him or her around the room to meet others. This is a great first step in helping the person of the minority culture feel accepted.

- *Intentionality.* Jesus expressed his love for all people by encountering the Samaritan woman and engaging her in conversation. "A man who has friends must himself be friendly" (Prov. 18:24 NKJV).

- *Risking rejection.* Because speaking with this woman was against his cultural tradition, Jesus risked being rejected by his disciples. Jesus was rejected by many whom he encountered. Experiencing the final act of rejection on the cross, Jesus prayed, "Father, forgive them, for they do not know what they are doing" (Luke 23:34). Yes, if you try to develop friendships with those of a different race or culture, you might experience rejection, but it's better to have tried and failed than not to have tried at all.

- *Respect.* Jesus demonstrated respect by speaking to the Samaritan woman despite Jewish tradition. He treated her as a person of worth.
- *Forgiveness.* Whatever the historical differences between the Jews and Samaritans, Jesus dismissed them, not letting those differences hinder a cross-cultural relationship.
- *Overcoming our fear of other cultures with our Christlike faith.* Jesus did not appear to be fearful when entering a Samaritan village. But we might be, which is natural. Don't let your nervousness imprison you. Prayer helps. God is with you, so feel free to talk with him.
- *Persevering.* Jesus did not let the Samaritan woman's initial rejection stop him from trying to get to know her.
- *Emotional healing.* Christ listened to this wounded woman. Often our listening communicates "I care about you. You are important."
- *Extending grace.* Jesus extended grace by not walking away after the woman rejected him. Rather, he offered to her what she did not deserve.
- *Patience.* Encountering a different culture might require time to observe and process differences.
- *Spending time together.* Spending quantity time with a person is often viewed as an act of respect and love. This is especially true with people of color. Quality time comes out of quantity time. It is often during this quantity time that God gives us "aha" moments, which was

what the Samaritan woman experienced in her conversation with Jesus.

- *Serving others.* Jesus modeled serving others when he put the needs of the Samaritan woman ahead of his own. "Do nothing from selfishness or empty conceit, but with humility consider one another as more important than yourselves; do not merely look out for your own personal interests, but also for the interests of others" (Phil. 2:3–4 NASB). Expressing love in words and deeds that benefit the other person is loving as Jesus loved.
- *Mercy.* Jesus exhibited mercy by not condemning the woman but offering her forgiveness
- *Celebrating, not tolerating, other cultures.* By traveling into Samaria, speaking to the Samaritan woman, and eventually giving her eternal life, Jesus Christ modeled for us that all people are important. Another way of celebrating a different culture is to learn its history or its language.
- *Acts of service.* The entire encounter between Jesus and the Samaritan woman was an act of service. When this woman told her town about the good news of Jesus, she was healed of fear of rejection.

This is not an exhaustive list of the characteristics of loving those of a different race or culture. But loving as Jesus loved requires that we look beyond our own back yard and are willing to move into the world of those who are not like us. Our objective is to look out for the interests of others, to meet them where they are and seek to enrich their lives. That is certainly what Jesus did for the Samaritan woman. If we encounter injustice, we are to remember God's words to Israel: "Do not twist justice in legal matters by favoring the poor or being partial to the rich and powerful. Always judge people fairly" (Lev. 19:15 NLT). As Christ followers, we must do what is necessary to seek justice for all.

People are divided over whether systemic racism exists. Often our views and experiences shape our perspective on this question.

If we learn to address injustice when we see it and have the opportunity to do something about it, then our focus won't be on what others are or are not doing but instead will be on the situations in which we can have a positive impact for God's glory. God hates injustice, and so should we.

We also need to love the ones dispensing the injustice, because they too need God's love, just like those who experience injustice. We should hate the injustice, but not the ones being unjust. This requires God's supernatural love!

Remember the South Carolina church whose members forgave the white supremacist for killing their family members and friends. And the African American brother who forgave the White female police officer who killed his innocent brother, who was in his own apartment.

If we understand God's heart, then we know that interdependency is essential to the body of Christ. God's idea of interdependency requires that unity and diversity exist simultaneously, according to 1 Corinthians 12:12–27.

Ultimately, Jesus offered the Samaritan woman forgiveness for her failures, and eternal life. We also are to see all people as worthy of our time and attention. We may have the opportunity to point people to the God who loves them and wants to forgive their past and give them eternal life. God commands us to love others, and anything God commands is for our good. God also empowers us to do whatever he commands. The apostle Paul said, "I can do everything through Christ, who gives me strength" (Phil. 4:13 NLT).

We believe that the attitude expressed in loving behavior toward those of another race is the key to racial understanding, and will often lead to mutually beneficial and long-lasting friendships. We don't want you to just understand the concept of cross-cultural friendships; we want you to experience them! Our desire is that you will allow God to express his love to others through you. We believe that when the world sees Christians sincerely loving across racial and cultural lines, many people will be drawn to the one who loved them enough to die for them.

Your Thoughts

1. After reading this chapter, do you have a new perspective on loving like Jesus?
2. What impressed you most deeply about loving as he loved?
3. How do you envision yourself loving others cross-culturally as Jesus did?
4. What did you learn from Jesus' encounter with the Samaritan woman? How will Jesus' actions help you express God's love cross-culturally?

5. Will you ask God to lead you to someone of a different race or culture with whom you might begin a friendship?

CHAPTER 5

Friends Apologize and Forgive Each Other

(Clarence) It was like it happened yesterday, even though it was approximately twenty years ago. Unfortunately, some churches experience conflict or controversy. Our church was one of them. Our senior pastor, a good man, had what he thought was a tremendous idea, but it eventually caused some members to leave our church, including me.

I differed with our senior pastor's idea. Another member of our church, a person of color, an Asian man, also had concerns about our senior pastor's vision for our church's future. The Asian man and I met unintentionally at a YMCA while working out. He asked me how I felt about the conflict at church. Without demeaning our senior pastor, I expressed my concern. We had the same concerns. As we were about to go our separate ways, he said, "Let's do lunch sometime." I responded, "That sounds good."

I left and never gave lunch another thought. Unfortunately, probably like most Americans, I just figured his suggestion was something that is often said but seldom meant, similar to when someone asks you in public, "How are you doing?" Many of us say, "Fine." We have no desire to share how we really feel, nor do we really want to take time to hear how they are doing. It is simply a way of being polite, but not really engaging. John Powell, in his book *Why Am I Afraid to Tell You Who I Am?* refers to this as the first level of communication, which basically has no meaning, no degree of transparency. You can share this first level with anyone.

A few months later, this man asked me again about lunch and I gave the same response. After more time passed, I received a three- or four-page email telling me of my arrogance and other unimpressive qualities that he felt I possessed. Not being spiritually mature, I defended myself instead of realizing that he was wounded.

After receiving another email from him, I arranged a face-to-face meeting. He came to my house. We walked around my neighborhood and talked. Nothing was resolved; in fact, he became angrier, and so did I.

The last time I ever saw him was years ago at his home. He and his wife hosted some event to which Brenda and I were invited. His wife really wanted Brenda there or I'm pretty sure that I would not have been invited. This man and I were polite with each other. And that was it.

I would like to think that had I been a counselor like I am today, I would have put my ego aside to hear this man's pain.

Reassessing this painful encounter, I believe one cause

of our conflict was a cultural misunderstanding. When he suggested that we go to lunch, he was actually inviting me.

Another factor was my incredible ego at that time. I was working for a prestigious Christian organization. In my mind, I was a great man—or at least on my way to being a great man. If someone wanted to have lunch with me, unless I really wanted to spend time with them, that person better initiate lunch with me. He did not, so I didn't think he was serious. And I also thought he was okay with that.

Two additional cultural issues could have been involved: (1) because I was older than him, he might have expected me to initiate a lunch meeting out of respect to me as the elder in our relationship, and (2) because I was the American-born man, possibly he saw me as the host, and so I was to initiate our lunch meeting. I was so clueless and, regrettably, so self-centered at the time.

Neither one of us was spiritually mature enough to try to find the source of our conflict. It would have been great if one of us had been an adult about it, even for a brief moment. We might have become good friends. I might have been able to serve him, because he was having problems at home.

This amazingly intelligent man might have been lonely and might have been crying out to me for help. Maybe he felt that as a man of color, I would know how he felt about being accepted by the White culture. I don't think he was able to say to me, "I need help," or, "I'm lonely for friendship with another man, especially a man of color."

I'd like to think that if our paths ever crossed again, I would be spiritually mature enough to ask him for his forgiveness.

So there is my story of how to kill a cross-cultural friendship before it starts. Hopefully, you are more spiritually mature and more in tune with possible cultural differences than I was.

(Gary) I have long believed that there can be no long-term healthy relationships without apology and forgiveness. I say this for one reason: none of us is perfect! Friendships do not require perfection, but we must deal effectively with our failures. When we hurt a friend, intentionally or unintentionally, we create an emotional barrier between us. That barrier does not go away with the passing of time. It is removed only when we apologize and they choose to forgive us. If we have been offended by a friend and they do not offer an apology, then we should lovingly confront them, and if they apologize, we should freely forgive them. Jesus made this approach very clear when he said, "If your brother or sister sins against you, rebuke them; and if they repent, forgive them" (Luke 17:3). When someone apologizes to us, we should forgive them as God forgives us when we confess our sins.

This is God's formula for building healthy long-term friendships. But we do not always follow God's plan. Sometimes, because of our spiritual immaturity, selfishness, and pride, we do not apologize for our poor behavior. And for those same reasons, we are reluctant to forgive when someone apologizes to us. Cross-cultural friendships have the added ingredient of misunderstanding the cultural meanings of certain words and behaviors. Clarence's story illustrates how a possible friendship was killed before it started by misunderstanding, selfishness, and pride. Have you ever destroyed a potential friendship by similar behavior?

(Clarence) As a diversity consultant, relationship counselor, speaker, and, most important, married man, one of my favorite metaphors is this: *Communication is to marriage what location is to real estate. You've got to communicate, communicate, communicate. Assume nothing and talk about everything! Ask questions!* I wish I had learned this lesson much earlier in my life.

(Gary) As Clarence and I have reflected on cross-cultural friendships, we have come to the following conclusions:

- When in a cross-cultural encounter, take what is said as literal, unless the person tells you otherwise. When in doubt, ask for clarification.
- We can be hurt by something the other person does or doesn't do.
- We can unintentionally hurt another person because of our spiritual immaturity or focusing only on ourselves.
- An apology and forgiveness can restore the relationship—a prerequisite for any long-term friendship.
- Serving the other person and thinking of their well-being is a critical foundation for a friendship. Philippians 2:3–5 (NLT) says, "Don't be selfish; don't try to impress others. Be humble, thinking of others as better than yourselves. Don't look out only for your own interests, but take an interest in others, too. You must have the same attitude that Christ Jesus had."
- What can happen in a friendship of the same race is even more likely to happen cross-culturally, because we may be using the same words but speaking a totally different language. It is always wise to clarify what the other person means by what they say.

A Happier Ending

(Clarence) Some years ago, I attended a men's ministry training in Denver sponsored by Chuck Stecker, president of A Chosen Generation. While there, I ran into a Colorado Springs acquaintance, Craig Glass, a Caucasian, who had been a missionary and now leads Peregrine, an incredible ministry to men.

During a break at this all-day training, Craig said to me (or at least this is what I heard through my filters), "Clarence, I would like for us to be friends because I've always had a Black man in my life." My initial thought was, "If you need a Black friend, certainly any Black man will do. You don't necessarily need me. What new kind of racism is this?" I was furious, but I kept my composure. I don't remember what I said, but it wasn't positive. Avoiding Craig the remainder of the day and in the future became one of my priorities. This was difficult because we had a mutual friend, Vince, another men's ministry guy, who frequently had both of us speak at his men's group.

I was mad with Craig for about a year. Then the Holy Spirit began to consistently bring Craig to my mind. The Holy Spirit asked me to consider Craig's perspective. When I get upset, seldom if ever do I think of the other person's perspective or wonder whether there could even be another perspective.

As the Holy Spirit softened my heart, I did begin to try to understand Craig's perspective. Nothing came to mind except that he could have been sincere. The idea of Craig being sincere convicted me that my response to him was wrong. I owed him an apology.

I finally apologized to Craig. He graciously forgave me. We didn't become best friends. But we did move our relationship as acquaintances toward becoming friends.

A few years later, Craig and I decided to attend an event in Denver. I offered to drive so I could get to know him better. After I arrived at Craig's house, he invited me inside because he needed to finish a task in his office. As I looked around his study, I saw several pictures of him with African American men. Seeing that I noticed his pictures, he said, "Clarence, African American men have spoken powerfully into my life. This was one reason I asked you to be in my life." I was humbled and embarrassed.

Craig and I continued to run into each other, especially at the swimming pool at the YMCA. Craig is an outstanding swimmer, often winning the gold medal at the Colorado State Games. I asked him to help me with my swimming technique. I had good strokes, but I didn't know how to breathe in rhythm with my strokes. He helped me so much and even gave Andrea, one of my daughters, a few lessons.

But the story doesn't end there. I live in Colorado, a state with beautiful rivers. When I turned sixty, there were two water activities that I wanted to do while I was living in Colorado: whitewater rafting and fly fishing. I scratched fly fishing because I don't like flying insects. But I did get the opportunity to go whitewater rafting. When I went, the river was twice as high as normal, moving twice as fast, and I was in a raft full of novices. We hit a rock below the surface and I fell into the water. I remembered what the guide said to do to survive, but it was based on your ability to swim. When I resurfaced, my strokes and my ability to breathe while swimming enabled me to get back to the raft. To this day, I believe God used Craig to save my life. I've told Craig this.

Recently Craig asked me if we could try to figure out some way to do ministry together, especially in the area of improving race relations. I said, "Yes!" Now we're ministering together to promote and improve cross-cultural friendships.

What I Learned from This Experience

I learned from this experience that through my apologizing, God used the person to whom I apologized to indirectly save my life. That was sobering! Who would think that such a small step of obedience would save their life?

After my asking for Craig's forgiveness and his accepting my apology, God took our friendship to another level: we're becoming best friends. God has given us a long-term friendship.

(Gary) As this story demonstrates, apology and forgiveness can open the door to a meaningful friendship. A few years ago, I teamed up with Dr. Jennifer Thomas to write a book on how to make meaningful apologies. In our counseling, both of us had discovered that people have different ideas on how to express a sincere apology. So our research led us to ask thousands of people across America two questions: When you apologize, what do you typically say or do? When someone apologizes to you, what do you expect to hear them say or do? Their answers fell into five categories, and we later called them the five languages of apology.[3]

Typically, we learn to apologize, or not to apologize, from our parents. But because we have different parents than the person to whom we need to apologize, we likely have different ideas on how to apologize. We discovered that 10 percent of the population almost never apologizes. Most of these people are men who learned from their fathers that real men don't apologize. These men often leave a trail of broken relationships. As we noted earlier, none of us is perfect. If we don't apologize for our failures, we will not have close long-lasting friendships.

Here is a brief description of the five languages of apology. See whether one or more of these is what you consider to be a sincere apology:

1. *Expressing regret.* "I'm sorry." But don't ever use just those words alone. Tell them what you are sorry for. "I'm sorry that I lost my temper and spoke harshly to you." And don't ever use the word *but:* "I'm sorry that I lost my temper, but if you had not . . . then I would not . . ." Now you are no longer apologizing, but you are blaming them for your poor behavior.

2. *Accepting responsibility.* "I was wrong. I should not have done that. There is no excuse for what I did. I take full responsibility." Some people have difficulty admitting that they were wrong. Often, these individuals have grown up in homes where they received verbal putdowns as a child. Something in their mind says, "If I ever get to be an adult, I'll never be wrong again." They equate being wrong with being a bad person. But accepting responsibility for your behavior is a sign of strength, not weakness.

3. *Offering to make restitution.* "I know that I have hurt you. What can I do to make things right? How can I make this up to you? You don't deserve what I did. I want to make things right." If this is a person's apology language, they will always have an idea of what you can do. When you do it, they see your sincerity and will find it easier to forgive you.

4. *Expressing the desire to change.* "I don't want to keep doing this. I know—I did the same thing last month, and the month before that. I'm sick of doing this. Can you help me find a plan so I will not do this again?" If this is a person's apology language, they will help you find a plan. When you follow the plan and change your behavior, they will freely forgive you.

5. *Requesting forgiveness.* "Will you forgive me? I hope you can find it in your heart to forgive me. I value our friendship and I hope you can forgive me." For some people, this is an important part of a sincere apology. If you don't request forgiveness, in their mind, you have not apologized.

Most of us have one or two of these five that we consider necessary in expressing a sincere apology. In close relationships like marriage or deep friendships, people often have different apology languages. By nature, we express an apology in the language we would like to hear when others apologize to us. We speak our own apology language rather than the apology language of the person we have offended. This is why apologies often seem lame to us and make it harder for us to extend forgiveness. In close friendships, we learn to speak each other's apology language, making it easier to forgive each other. (You may wish to take the free apology quiz at 5lovelanguages.com to discover your apology language and then share it with your friend.)

Why Cross-Cultural Misunderstandings Can Happen More Easily and More Often

When we apologize to someone of a different culture, communicating sincerity might be even more difficult. One time, I was in China lecturing on the five languages of apology. I was told that in China, a common way to apologize is to purchase a meaningful gift for the person you have offended. Words aren't necessarily spoken. In giving the gift, you are communicating that you know you have offended them and you want to be forgiven. Shame is avoided in Chinese culture, so perhaps giving a gift is a way to avoid the shame of admitting that you did something wrong. This method of apologizing might fit in the broad category of making restitution, but in American culture, a gift needs to be accompanied by at least one of the other apology languages.

In cross-cultural friendships, we would do well to discuss what each of us considers to be a sincere apology. We need to learn how to apologize in a way that is meaningful to the other person. You might simply say, "I know that our parents typically teach us to apologize. My parents taught me to say, 'I'm sorry. I should not have done that.' What did your parents teach you to say when you apologize?"

The Power of Forgiveness

Apology alone does not restore a friendship. There must be a response to the apology. Forgiveness is the only response that removes the barrier created by the offense.

In the Old and New Testaments, there are three Hebrew words and four Greek words that are translated "forgive" or "forgiveness." The basic meaning of these words is twofold: "to pardon" and "to take away." To pardon is to grant mercy rather than demand justice. It is to lift the penalty for the offense. To take away is the choice to remove the barrier that was created by the offense. When forgiveness is extended, the pathway is opened to continue developing our friendship. If we refuse to forgive, the emotional barrier remains and the friendship does not move forward.

An African American man loaned five thousand dollars to a White man whom he considered a friend. The White man promised to pay it back with interest. But he invested the money in a business venture that failed. He could not find another job and was living on welfare. He apologized to his African American friend and admitted that he had made a poor financial decision. He told him that he hoped he would be able to repay him sometime in the future. His friend chose to forgive him and they continued to be friends. It was five years before the loan was repaid, but in those five years, their friendship grew even deeper. That is the power of forgiveness.

There are some things that forgiveness does not do. Forgiveness does not remove the memory of the offense. You may have heard someone say, "If you have not forgotten, you have not forgiven." That is not true. Everything that has ever happened to us is stored in our brains. With the passing of time, some events slip into the subconscious mind and we seldom think of them. But from time to time, the memory of the offense may jump back into the conscious mind. The memory of what happened is often accompanied by emotions—anger, hurt, sadness, or other emotions. So what do we do when the memory and emotions return after we have chosen forgiveness? I believe we should share our memories and emotions with God. We might pray, "Lord, you know what I am remembering and the emotions that I am feeling today, but I thank you that I have forgiven that offense. So help me to do something loving toward this person today." We don't allow the memory and the emotions to control our behavior. We don't choose our emotions, but we do choose our behavior. Loving words or actions enhance friendship.

In cross-cultural friendships, we will sometimes do or say things that offend the other person. Often it may be unintentional, such as the time I called James and Clarence boys. At that stage in my life, I had no thought that the term *boy* was offensive to African Americans. If I had been defensive and not taken time to listen to their perspective and then sincerely apologize, our relationship might have ended before it got started. Their willingness to forgive me allowed our relationship to continue.

> We don't choose our emotions, but we do choose our behavior. Loving words or actions enhance friendship.

We strongly suggest that when developing friendships with those of a different race or culture, you express the following sentiment early in the relationship:

"If I ever offend you by something I say or do, or something I fail to say or do, please tell me. I want our relationship to be open and honest. If I offend you, I want to understand it and apologize. Can we agree on this kind of openness?"

Such an agreement opens the door to a close personal friendship. Remember, there can be no long-term healthy relationships without apology and forgiveness.

Your Thoughts

1. Do you remember the last time you had to apologize to someone? What was it for?

2. Did that person forgive you? If he or she did, how did that make you feel?

3. If you were forgiven, did that take your friendship to a deeper level? Why or why not?

4. When was the last time someone apologized to you? How did you feel when they apologized? Did you forgive them? Why or why not?

5. If you forgave that person, did your friendship go to a deeper level? Why or why not?

6. Have you ever had to grant forgiveness in a cross-cultural friendship? What was hard about that situation? What helped overcome the hurt?

7. If you ever had to ask for forgiveness in a cross-cultural friendship, how did you do it? How would you do it differently after reading this chapter?

CHAPTER 6

Friends Are Not Colorblind

(Clarence) After I was introduced to an audience by the president of a Christian nonprofit that hired me to conduct my Maximizing Difference (biblical diversity) training, a White gentleman shouted, "I'm colorblind. I don't see color."

I have been a diversity consultant to faith-based and secular organizations for nearly twenty-five years. A diversity consultant helps organizations that desire to be more diverse to reach that goal by evaluating the organizations' situation, providing training to create or increase awareness, and equipping the organizations with doable practical methods to improve and maintain diversity.

The White gentleman's proclamation that he was colorblind is a statement I often hear, frequently in the very first session of my diversity training.

Some people saying this have the best of intentions. In

my experience, the majority of these people are Caucasian. But even some people of color feel just as strongly about being colorblind. Some who use this term are trying to communicate that they see no difference in the cultures or that they treat everyone as their equal. Or that they wish there were no visible differences between people of different cultures or races.

Others use this term as a defense mechanism to suggest that they are not prejudiced. They do not want to be associated with or blamed for any racial injustice.

If you have expressed this statement, let me assure you, my response is in no way intended to offend. But will you consider a different perspective than being colorblind? My hope is that you will prayerfully contemplate what these words imply. I am fully aware that my decades in diversity training doesn't mean that my perspective is necessarily correct, but I do believe it is worth considering.

A Different Perspective

The word *colorblind* in the context of culture or race relations can be unintentionally misleading and may stimulate negative emotions and raise serious questions, such as, If you don't see color, does that mean that in your eyes all people are White? Or Black? Or some other color?

When I hear "I'm colorblind" in one of my sessions, I typically ask that individual to identify the color of the clothes he or she is wearing. They have no problem telling me, which leads to another question: "If you can distinguish the color of your clothes, why do you say that you are colorblind?" They admit they are not actually colorblind. Next, I ask, "Why do you want to be colorblind?"

I understand that the intentions of those who say "I'm colorblind" are usually good and honorable. They don't see skin color as being a relationship issue, nor do they want it to be an issue. I'm just suggesting that using the word *colorblind* may imply that we are all the same. In reality we are racially and culturally different. The goal is not uniformity but unity. God brings together people of all races and cultures and makes them one in

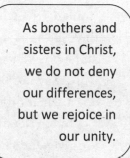

As brothers and sisters in Christ, we do not deny our differences, but we rejoice in our unity.

Christ. We are united as brothers and sisters, and we all call him Father. We do not deny our differences, but we rejoice in our unity. Our differences actually lead us to unity.

What Does the Bible Teach about Difference?

God revealed himself as the Creator. His creativity celebrates diversity. We are told that no two snowflakes are exactly alike. In Genesis 1, notice that after God made the heavens and the earth, creation was formless, empty, and dark before he began his creative work. Then God created light and darkness, day and night. Next God created a space between the waters of the heavens and the waters of the earth. God called the space sky. Then he created vegetation and animals.

His last creation was a human being—us. We are often called the crown of God's creation because we are made in his image. Humankind was given meaningful work caring for God's creatures. God prepared a livable place for human beings, providing for their physical needs. Notice: God did not create two men or two women; he created a man and a woman, who tend to be radically different from each other in their physical anatomy, mental processing, physical strength, and more. When a man and a woman are united in a relationship, they are better together for God's glory than they are apart. Their differences are to be celebrated, not denied.

In the New Testament, we discover that not all Christians are given the same spiritual gifts. The Holy Spirit gives different gifts to different believers. We all are gifted and are to use our gifts to accomplish God's purposes (1 Cor. 12:4–7). A great diversity of gifts are given for a united purpose.

Why Difference Is Essential in God's Design

So, in creation, and in our spiritual gifts, we see that God created diversity. Later, the apostle Paul gives us a picture of why diversity is so significant in the body of Christ. He uses the human body as an illustration of how the Christian family is made up of great diversity, but each part is vital.

> The human body has many parts, but the many parts make up one whole body. So it is with the body of Christ. Some of us are Jews, some are Gentiles, some are slaves, and some

are free. But we have all been baptized into one body by one Spirit, and we all share the same Spirit.

Yes, the body has many different parts, not just one part. If the foot says, "I am not a part of the body because I am not a hand," that does not make it any less a part of the body. And if the ear says, "I am not part of the body because I am not an eye," would that make it any less a part of the body? If the whole body were an eye, how would you hear? Or if your whole body were an ear, how would you smell anything?

But our bodies have many parts, and God has put each part just where he wants it. How strange a body would be if it had only one part! Yes, there are many parts, but only one body.

—1 CORINTHIANS 12:12–20 NLT

Paul clearly applies this concept to racial and cultural differences when he says, "Some of us are Jews, some are Gentiles, some are slaves, and some are free," but we are all part of one body and each of us has an essential role to play. None of us should aspire to be like other parts of the body but should seek to play our role for the benefit of the whole. We are not to be colorblind but to thank God for our divine differences and that together we are the body of Christ.

Paul then says,

The eye can never say to the hand, "I don't need you." The head can't say to the feet, "I don't need you."

In fact, some parts of the body that seem weakest and least important are actually the most necessary. And the parts we regard as less honorable are those we clothe with the greatest care. So we carefully protect those parts that should not be seen, while the more honorable parts do not require this special care. So God has put the body together such that extra honor and care are given to those parts that have less dignity. This makes for harmony among the members, so that all the members care for each other. If one part suffers, all the parts suffer with it, and if one part is honored, all the parts are glad.

All of you together are Christ's body, and each of you is a part of it.

—1 CORINTHIANS 12:21–27 NLT

Clearly, God highly values diversity. He doesn't want us all to be the same.

According to these verses, God has created our differences to glorify himself. He wants us to embrace difference and each other. These verses powerfully teach that God desires his followers to live out interdependency with others in his body because this unity glorifies him. Respect for our differences leads to acceptance of each other's roles in the body of Christ. Thus, we can learn from each other. We need each other. When Brenda and I got married, she let me write our vows. One statement I wrote was, "We're better together for God's glory than we are apart." I believe this is also true in the church. Our differences are designed for our good and God's glory.

If you change the phrase "more honorable parts" to "majority culture," does this influence your perspective regarding "helping those who require special care," especially if the phrase "minority culture" or "people of color in America" is substituted for "helping those who require special care"? Why or why not? What are the implications of this perspective?

How do you know when people of another culture or race are being treated with less dignity than you? How do you know when someone of another culture requires special care or is suffering or is honored? How do you know when they are hitting roadblocks, experiencing injustice, or living in poverty? How do you know when and how to help? I believe the answers lie in building close personal friendships across racial and cultural lines. As Christians we recognize that God's family is composed of people of many races and cultures. Reflect on the following verses:

> Respect for our differences leads to acceptance of each other's roles in the body of Christ.

- "In that day the Root of Jesse will stand as a banner for the peoples; the nations will rally to him, and his resting place will be glorious" (Isa. 11:10). Notice the words *peoples* and *nations.*
- "I . . . am about to come and gather the people of all nations and languages, and they will come and see my glory" (Isa. 66:18).
- "And with your blood you purchased for God persons from every tribe and language and people and nation" (Rev. 5:9).
- "After this I looked, and there before me was a great multitude that no one could count, from every nation, tribe, people and language, standing before the throne and

before the Lamb. They were wearing white robes and were holding palm branches in their hands" (Rev. 7:9).

If we are going to spend eternity together, why would we not want to be friends while on earth? It seems to me that one of God's goals for his followers is to learn to understand and embrace differences. This is what the Bible teaches. This is why my diversity training program is titled Maximizing Difference. As Christ followers, we should be drawn to difference, rather than ignoring or minimizing it.

How Can We Embrace Difference?

According to Ephesians 4:3, Christ followers are commanded to "make every effort to keep yourselves united in the Spirit, binding yourselves together with peace" (NLT). Verse 2 of this chapter tells us how: "Be patient with each other, making allowance for each other's faults because of your love." If we substitute the word *uniqueness* for "faults," we will build the unity that God desires for his body. Being patient and making allowances for our differences is the road to building true friendships.

My first trip to West Africa was with Sports Ambassadors' Christian basketball team. On this trip, I learned the importance of this verse. We were playing Nigeria's national basketball team. In our prep session about African culture, we were told that if a man likes you purely as a friend, he may just grab your hand and hold it as you walk together. We were told not to pull our hands away because this would be a huge insult to that person.

God-Designed Difference	Man's Colorblindness
May make you uncomfortable	Comfortable
Requires faith	Doesn't require faith
Requires interdependency	Doesn't require interdependency
Promotes unity	Doesn't promote unity
Honors individuals	Promotes sameness
About others	About me
Unlimited creativity[4]	Limited creativity

This was such a foreign concept to me until a member of the Nigerian army basketball team grabbed my hand as we walked down the street. As uncomfortable and weird as I felt, I did not withdraw my hand. I was learning to be patient and make allowances for our cultural differences. Before we left the country, this basketball player gave me numerous gifts. We stayed in touch after I returned to the United States. In the Christian family, we too must be patient and make allowance for our racial and cultural differences, even when they are uncomfortable to us.

What Does Colorblindness Imply?

I am sure that the word *colorblindness* means different things to different people. After all, that is the theme of this chapter—we are all different. As I said earlier, I believe that some people who use this word are trying to communicate that they don't want race or culture to be an issue in relationships. I applaud their intent. But if we don't recognize and share racial and cultural differences, how will we ever get to know one another? How can we build close personal relationships?

I have sometimes wondered whether those who use the word *colorblind* have a picture of everyone being the same. If so, which same do they envision? If I am African American, do I want everyone to be African American? Or if I am Caucasian, do I want everyone to be Caucasian? Should Native Americans want everyone to be Native American? Regardless, someone would have to make changes. Would it not be better for all of us to be who we are and to learn to understand and embrace our differences? Affirming and helping each other, we all grow in Christlikeness, which is the goal of all Christ followers. We are not the same. We are very different. But we seek to use our differences for each other's benefit. Then together, we share the love of Christ with those who do not yet know him.

How to Respond to Hearing *Colorblind*

No one enjoys a battle over vocabulary. Instead, I encourage you to remember courtesy when encountering those who say, "I am colorblind." Focus on sharing a better perspective rather than righting a wrong. Positive racial relationships grow when we acknowledge our differences and seek to learn from each other.

While writing this book, I met a Caucasian man who has become a good friend. During our first conversation, we talked about racial tensions in America. He said he was colorblind and that he once worked for an African American manager. He said he treated his African American manager like everyone else. My initial thought was, "If you're colorblind, how could you tell what color this manager was? And if you obviously were able to see that he was Black, what is the point of stating that you are colorblind when you obviously are not?" I liked this man and saw no need to share my perspective, which could have created an awkward moment at this social function. Perhaps we will continue this discussion in private in the future.

Normally, I don't say anything when a new acquaintance says the word *colorblind* in the context of race. I don't say anything because I don't have a relationship with that person. I have my perspective, but it might not be an appropriate setting in which to share it. Even if I'm asked to comment, I would assess the setting and ask God for wisdom in responding. Such a prayer is one way to show courtesy to the people God brings into your life. Close personal friendships provide the best setting to discuss this and all other differences.

The Power of Love

(Gary) Love begins with an attitude, and then finds expression in words and deeds. As I read this chapter by Clarence, I sensed his love for the reader. Love always respects the opinion of others when sharing your own. It has been this kind of love that has guided our friendship over these many years. I hope you have found this chapter helpful as you evaluate the concept of being colorblind as opposed to acknowledging and embracing differences. Close personal friendships dig deeper than casual conversations. In such friendships, we often discover differences, listen with empathy, and seek to learn from each other.

I found the analogy of the body to have huge implications for the Christian when it comes to cross-racial relationships. True Christians, regardless of racial or cultural differences, are one body. We are to be there for each other, mutually seeking to help each other move toward the goal of spiritual maturity. In my opinion, the Christian church does a fairly good job of helping other cultures at a distance. We give money and send food and supplies to fellow Christians and non-Christians both in our country and around the world. We don't do as well at identifying the needs of those who are close at hand. I think this is largely because we don't have close friendships with people of other races and cultures who are near us. Again, I ask, what would happen if every Christian had at least one close friend of another race or culture?

Your Thoughts

1. Have you ever used the word *colorblind?* If so, what were you trying to convey?
2. What were your initial thoughts regarding the word *colorblind* possibly being interpreted negatively?

3. Why do you think God seems to be a God of difference?

4. What do you think could be some possible dangers of the colorblind mindset?

5. According to 1 Corinthians 12:12–27, what are some of the possible dangers of not embracing God's design of difference as a follower of Christ?

6. Have you ever protected someone of another culture? What happened? How did you feel about it? Did others of your culture see it? How did they respond to your action? Did their response affirm or disappoint you? How did the person of the other culture respond to you? Did that individual's response affirm or disappoint you?

7. Have you ever intentionally said or implied that you didn't need someone of another culture? If so, why? Can you apologize to that person? Have you asked God for his forgiveness?

CHAPTER 7

Friends Disagree Agreeably

(Clarence) Several years ago, I had a friend, Roger (not his real name), with whom I couldn't come to an agreement. We were both Christians and worked together for a conservative Christian organization.

I was the first person of color to work in management at this organization. I did not have the same political views of this organization, but the leaders said that they wanted to reach people who did not look like them and that political differences were fine.

They really weren't.

Roger and I prayed together periodically at work. He was concerned about the subtle racism he saw me experiencing at this organization.

But Roger and I disagreed about politics.

We never argued about our different political views, but

no matter how much Roger and I disagreed, I don't think we ever changed the other's mind.

Because of Roger's and my love for Christ and for each other, and because of our times of praying together, whenever Roger shared a political viewpoint that I disagreed with, I listened. Not only did I listen but I researched it as fairly as I knew how. I did this because I also respected Roger. We learned to disagree agreeably, and we had a healthy workplace friendship.

Roger was a workplace friend, but even close friends will inevitably disagree on any number of issues. This can be especially true of cross-cultural relationships. To avoid conflict is to avoid reality. To avoid reality hampers a healthy, honest, intimate, and transparent relationship. Disagreements open the door for meaningful conversation. The goal is not to avoid conflicts but to use them to enhance the relationship.

Poet James Baldwin's words inform us of what is necessary for developing a friendship that will last, especially a cross-cultural one in which the unknown and a lack of trust can be tremendous obstacles:

> I think you owe it to me, as *my friend*, to fight me, to let me get away with nothing, to force me to be clear, to force me to be honest, to allow me to take no refuge in rage or in despair . . . and of course, I owe you the same. This means *we are certainly going to hurt each other's feelings from time to time.* But that's one of the ways in which *people learn from each other.*[5]

Baldwin's words describe a realistic picture of genuine friendship. Obviously, we don't get to this kind of friendship overnight. It takes time and effort, but it's the kind of friend-ship that endures and uses conflict as a platform for growth.

(Gary) If we handle conflict in a constructive manner, it will deepen our friendship. But if our approach is argumen-tative, with each trying to win the argument, it will fracture our relationship. Instead, we can embrace conflict as a normal part of friendship. We would like to suggest ways to make conflict resolution easier. First, we want to share a real-life conflict between Clarence's daughter, Andrea Shuler, and her long-time White friend Elise.

Here is their account in their own words.

> **Andrea:** Elise and I met in college. Both of us had the same major, joined the same parachurch campus group, went to the same church, and participated in the same internship. It would have been impossible for us not to meet. Needless to say, we got to know each other very well. During my college years, I went through a brief season of couch surfing. She and her roommates rented one of the houses that I rotated through. Elise and I have tremendous respect for each other. We always seem to bless each other whenever we talk. Our talks have been more frequent due to the fact that racial injustice is more visible now.

> **Elise:** I have been on my equity learning journey for the last few years. My background is in social work, and I participate in a few different racial reconciliation and equity groups, and I still make a lot of missteps. As a White person in this work who is trying to

understand her biases and blind spots, there is always a lot to learn. I live in the western part of the United States and have been more proximate to indigenous groups and tribes. I have been learning about Native American issues. Part of that learning is associated with cultural appropriation and erasure of tribes. Another part is related to the character of Pocahontas, which Disney has appropriated.

Andrea: For years, Elise has been so loving and supportive of me. So imagine my surprise when she sent an Instagram DM that was initially friendly but concluded by shaming me! I had posted a picture of the Halloween costumes a friend and I wore. We both dressed as Pocahontas. A few days after Halloween, I received Elise's disapproving message. In her effort to educate me, she attached an article titled "My Culture Is Not Your or Your Kids' Halloween Costume." Can you imagine my reaction?! I had so many thoughts and questions simultaneously. Why was my picture offensive? I realized that I needed to wait and to take into consideration that this message came from a friend. "Why is my friend mad at me? But she 'liked' my post. Should I take it down? I don't want to be insensitive. I'm only showing respect for Pocahontas. Doesn't that make it less offensive and understandable?"

I am aware that there are many problems with how Pocahontas's given name and story have been changed and characterized. In the fifth grade, I learned that she was a real person and that her story was much worse than how Disney portrayed it. I was conflicted even then, because I had loved the movie years prior, then discovered it was a distorted version. Nonetheless, I've always loved Pocahontas as a Disney princess. She was also one of the few I could imitate in my childhood because she was a person of color. So I took some time to process how I should respond to Elise. Here is my partial reply: "I actually am part Native American. My great-great-grandmother on my mother's side was Cherokee and my father's side of the family is also related to Cherokees." It was necessary for Elise to realize that "as a Black person, I have my own feelings about people's dress and mimicking how African Americans speak."

Elise: After receiving Andrea's response on Instagram, I reached out to check in with her. She asked for a phone call to discuss things. So we connected a few days later. She was able to share what had been hurtful to her. My sending that article had felt condescending and my short message felt shaming. I owned that and apologized. I shared with Andrea the true story of Pocahontas (who was actually named Matoaka). She is considered one of the first of many Missing and Murdered Indigenous Women (#MMIW), and her story has been maligned and twisted by dominant culture via Disney.

Andrea: Elise had a valid concern. She knew that First Nations people or Native Americans are hurt by those wearing Pocahontas costumes on Halloween.

We went back and forth a few times in efforts to defend our perspectives. My uneasiness kept increasing because of the direction our dialogue was taking. So I retreated from our conversation. I hated feeling the way I felt. But even more, I hated the rift that had come between Elise and me. She had been such a solid friend! We agreed to talk again in a few days, but we each knew that we still disagreed.

Allowing a few days to pass was so wise. She sent me a text that requested the continuation of our conversation and gave me the option to drop it. I was moved that she reached out to resolve our issue. Elise was right; we hadn't finished. We set a time to talk by phone instead of texting or messaging. But when the time for our talk was near, I was incredibly nervous. Here we were, two women, one White, one Black, who had been friends for twelve years, having a disagreement over another race of people!

Elise and I were able to work through our differences by listening to each other. I began our conversation by letting her know how I felt when I received her message and article. She interrupted me to apologize. She admitted that sending an article was not the best way to educate someone, especially someone like me. Elise's approach came across as cold and shameful. A phone call might have saved days of angst. Because of our long friendship, I naturally forgave her. In the same sentence, I told her that I appreciated her passion for people as well as her boldness to be an advocate for people of color. I asked her for more information about indigenous people and her recent findings. The phone call was an effective and loving way to talk, hear each other's tones, and ask questions about each other's comments. Neither of us was defensive or tried to be right or justify our actions. Through this encounter, we have helped each other approach other situations differently. For example, Elise told me that as a result of our poor communication, she learned to communicate with an acquaintance who had a different perspective. She didn't send them literature to read as a means of correction. Instead, they talked with each other about the issue.

I decided to leave the picture of my Pocahontas costume on my profile because I do share a cultural relationship to First Nations people or Native Americans. After our conversation, Elise understood this. I love culture, and the post now reminds me to do my research and consider how others might interpret images, statements, and phrases despite my intention.

I'm grateful to Elise for walking with me through this process. I am thankful we repaired damage to our friendship. Above all, I am glad that God's Spirit permeated our talk. Jesus Christ has been and will remain the foundation for both of us.

We both learned that when you have a conflict with a friend:

- Don't use social media to attempt to resolve a conflict or disagreement.
- Pray before reaching out to your friend.
- Reach out to your friend; don't wait for your friend to reach out to you first.
- Communicate face to face or at the very least by phone in order to hear the other person's tone of voice.
- When you do meet face to face or talk via phone, don't be defensive.
- Your friendship is more important than the disagreement.
- Be open to learning.
- Embrace complexity.
- Ask questions instead of making assumptions.
- Humbly challenge your friend with the goal of learning and growing together, while caring for each other.
- Conclude your time together by praying together.

(Gary) There are three primary ways to resolve a conflict in a cross-cultural friendship, all of which require empathetic listening, by which I mean a sincere effort to put yourself in the shoes of the other person to try to see the world through their eyes. Only then can we come to a satisfactory resolution of our differences. Once we have heard each other's perspective, we can honestly say, "I think I understand what you are saying, and I can see how that makes sense. So how can we solve our conflict?" Now we can focus on finding a solution rather than trying to win an argument.

The first possible solution was illustrated in the story about Andrea and Elise. I call this option I Will Meet You on Your Side. Elise learned something about Andrea that she had not known earlier—that Andrea had ancestral roots with indigenous people. Her identity with them was positive and in no way demeaning. So Elise was able to understand and embrace Andrea's liberty (freedom, right) to keep her Pocahontas Halloween costume on her profile if she wished. She was willing to meet Andrea on her side and no longer condemn her. Their process to reach a satisfactory solution to their conflict was fraught with tension, and they each learned much about how they might have done it better. But they reached a positive solution and their friendship not only survived but was deepened.

The second option is I Will Meet You in the Middle. Neither of us can quite bring ourselves to go to the other's side, but we can find a meeting place in the middle of our opposing views. Here's an example of meeting in the middle: David and Catrell had an interracial marriage. David was White and Catrell was Black. The first Christmas after they were married, they had a huge argument. David's parents lived in one state, and Catrell's in another. David wanted them to spend Christmas with his family. Catrell wanted them to spend Christmas with her parents. After heated arguments, they decided to get counseling. The counselor assured them that theirs was a common conflict among young marrieds whose parents live hundreds of miles apart. The counselor first shared that each of their desires were normal because we typically have an emotional bond with our family of origin, especially if we have good family relationships.

Then the counselor helped them explore various possibilities. Perhaps they could decide not to go to either set of parents for Christmas but start their own Christmas tradition. Perhaps they could spend Christmas with one set of parents and Thanksgiving with the other, with the understanding that the following year they would switch the order. They discussed other options, but alternating holidays is the one on which they agreed. They met in the middle. It was not what either of them originally wanted, but it did seem fair to them. Of course, then the question was which set of parents gets the first Christmas visit. They talked about flipping a coin, but later agreed that since Catrell's parents were older and having some physical problems, they would visit her parents the first Christmas. (In this detail, David met Catrell on her side.)

The third option is We Disagree Agreeably. This is illustrated by Clarence's workplace friendship with Roger. In the early stages of their friendship, they discussed politics. But it became evident that they were never going to convince the other to change their political views. However, because they were both committed to Christ, respected each other as brothers in Christ, and enjoyed their friendship, they simply agreed to disagree but not allow their political differences to derail their friendship.

Conflicts in cross-cultural friendships can be resolved in one of these three ways. But as noted earlier, solutions require a commitment to understanding and learning from each other. When we take this approach, we will not allow our differences to divide us. Rather, they will be pathways to enhancing our friendship.

Why Cross-Cultural Conflicts Happen More Easily

(Clarence) It seems to be easier for cross-cultural relationships to have conflict because we may often be using the same words but not speaking the same language. Let's consider a man and a woman who are dating. The man asks the woman out for dinner. He asks her where she wants to go for dinner. Her response: "Anywhere is fine." They drive to several restaurants. At each one, the woman says she doesn't feel like eating there. Eventually the man becomes frustrated because he took her comment literally—*anywhere* is fine. But she was thinking figuratively when she made her comment—translation: "I don't know what I'm in the mood for eating, but I'll know it when I see it." If the man takes the woman literally, but she is thinking figuratively, and neither confers with the other for clarity, conflict will almost certainly arise.

The same is true cross-culturally, as when the Asian gentleman in my church really meant that he wanted to have lunch with me, whereas I thought he was just being polite.

Not Knowing How We Are Different Creates Problems

(Clarence) Another factor in cross-cultural friendships is that different cultures respond to disagreement or conflict differently, and not understanding that can lead to unnecessary frustration and anger.

Dr. Martin Davidson, a professor at the Darden Business

School of the University of Virginia, did research that revealed that in general, Blacks and Whites respond differently to conflict.[6] In his research project, Dr. Davidson interviewed sixty African Americans and sixty Caucasians in an MBA program, seeking to determine how students from Black and White cultures responded to conflict. His conclusions revealed certain consistent responses that could be based on culture.

The following are some consistencies that surfaced:

- In heated conflicts, Whites are more comfortable backing off and giving distance to get under control and be rational before discussing the issue.
- African Americans generally expect to engage and have discussion, which is considered an issue of courtesy and respect. To walk away shows a lack of respect.
- Not only are these culturally different behaviorial patterns of withdrawal and engagement in heated conflicts significant, but how each participant interprets the behavior affects the relationship.
- Conflict plus subordination complicates the issue if a White must report to a Black and vice versa.

The first bullet point is such a critical cross-cultural observation. In general, Whites feel that if someone is emotional, that person is out of control and not rational. Again, in general, White culture attributes emotion to a lack of intelligence (unless at a sporting event). So if a person of color is being emotional (loud or physically expressive), from a White person's perspective, they are out of control and need to calm down before a rational solution can be discussed.

The second bullet suggests that although they are being expressive or emotional, or being themselves, people of African American culture usually want to resolve the issue immediately. For a White to walk away is to convey that the African American is out of control. The African American feels insulted and controlled.

The findings of this study may also apply to people of other cultures, such as First Nations people or Native Americans and Hispanics or Latinos. Or those groups may have their own generalities unique to their cultures.

An Attempt to Restore a Cross-Cultural Relationship

(Clarence) Following is a poem I wrote to a friend of a different culture with whom I'd had a heated conflict. The poem was my attempt to reconcile our friendship, and my friend appreciated receiving it.

A Friend for Always

In the meeting the other day,
You seemed to wipe a tear away.
I think because our hearts are so near,
You had some reasons to fear.
Though the future is certainly unclear,
A picture of my love for you will always be
    clear.

Our love for each other is not deserved,
But a gift from our Father above.
A gift from God is special indeed.
It is certain to him that it is each other we need.
Where the future takes us, we cannot say.
But our hearts will never be far away.
I love you because you are a friend for always.

How You Can Resolve a Conflict in a Cross-Cultural Friendship

To close this important chapter, let's review some of the key ideas we've discussed:

Three Ways to Resolve a Conflict in a Cross-Cultural Friendship

I Will Meet You on Your Side	Learn your friend's perspective and agree to go with their idea.
I Will Meet You in the Middle	Find a place between your opposing views.
We Disagree Agreeably	Respect each other and do not allow differences to derail your friendship.

So the next time you find yourself in conflict within a cross-cultural relationship, first pray, "Lord, please give me your wisdom to hear and understand my friend's perspective. Help me to remember that our relationship is more important than my being right or wrong." Or if you are both Christ followers, suggest that you pray together before trying to further resolve your conflict.

Next, remember that you both have different filters based on your culture and your experiences.

Serve your friend by allowing him or her to speak first while you focus on trying to understand what he or she is saying. Once you agree on what has been said, you can seek to be understood by sharing your perspective.

The goal of conflict is to gain understanding, not to win the conflict. If one of you *wins* the conflict, you both *lose* in the relationship. Understanding doesn't equal agreement, but it usually alleviates frustration. Often, understanding leads to agreement.

Don't avoid conflict. Conflict is normal in relationships. Conflict is an aspect of friendship. To avoid conflict is to avoid reality. The key is how we handle conflict. One benefit of conflict, if it is handled correctly, is that we learn that something is more important to our friend than we realized. They will learn the same about us. This information improves our friendship.

These suggestions can prove invaluable when encountering a cross-cultural conflict.

Your Thoughts

1. During your first conflict with a close personal friend, whether of the same or a different race or culture, what were your feelings?

2. Why do you think you had those feelings?

3. Would you have done anything differently if you were either Andrea or Elise? What would you have done and why?

4. What did you learn from Andrea and Elise about resolving a conflict, especially a cross-cultural one?

5. What did you learn from Dr. Davidson's interview of sixty Caucasian and sixty African American MBA students?

6. How did James Baldwin's words in this chapter impact your thinking about working through cross-cultural conflict?

CHAPTER 8

Friends Are Friends Forever

(Clarence) When I met Gary Chapman in 1968 as a fourteen-year-old, I had no idea that we would become friends. It was a particularly turbulent time with racial tension nationwide. Within approximately five years, a president, a presidential candidate, and the national leader for African Americans were all assassinated. I certainly didn't think that Gary and I would become friends—actually more like family—for the rest of our lives.

(Gary) I agree with Clarence. Neither of us had any idea in those early years that we would become lifelong friends. Our relationship began by simply treating each other with courtesy, showing respect, and relating in a friendly manner.

(Clarence) In chapter 1, when Gary took that first step onto the basketball court to meet Russell and me that evening at the church gym, he had a calmness, friendliness, safeness, and something just different about him. Much later, I realized it was the Holy Spirit working through Gary.

Someone has to take that first step to develop a cross-cultural friendship. In doing so, one risks rejection. But it's worth the risk because it could open the door to a lifelong friendship.

(Gary) Clarence credits me with taking the first step, but I think he took the first step by putting himself in a social setting with people of a different race. He may have been motivated by his love for basketball, his interest in girls, or his wanting to protect his friend Russell. He certainly did not show up at the gym to build a friendship with a White man a few years older than he. But cross-racial friendships cannot happen until we are in physical proximity. Once we encounter each other and treat each other with respect, the seeds of a possible friendship are planted. If we are open, God may well water those seeds until they become a lifelong friendship.

> Someone has to take that first step.

(Clarence) One discipleship principle that I've learned from Gary is that once you disciple someone, that relationship becomes a lifelong commitment. This is what he has taught me. He has never said this, but he has certainly modeled this principle for me and others. It seems like at every key moment in my life, Gary was there for me and will always be there for me.

After I became a Christ follower, Gary knew that I needed to learn about the Bible, so he invited me to his home weekly to teach me. Then he invited me to his weekly college Bible study, also held at his home. I think he did that to keep James and me out of trouble.

When I went to college, he had the college students from his Bible study write me. It was nice receiving letters in college (back when people wrote letters). I made quite a few friendships as I responded to them.

After college, I eventually went to seminary and earned a master of divinity degree, a necessary degree for most ministers. Gary and my late senior pastor Mark Corts were the ones who relentlessly encouraged me to get this degree.

> When you disciple someone, the relationship is a lifelong commitment.

Gary preached at my ordination service. Before preaching the sermon, he told the audience, "My children, Shelley and Derek, pray for Clarence every night. They consider him to be their big brother." It was at this point that tears rolled down my cheeks. I never knew this. Who was this guy who had his children praying for me?

Gary did the premarital counseling for Brenda and me. It was quite unique because he was in North Carolina, Brenda was in Texas, and I was in Oklahoma. I loved everything he was teaching us until he taught about submission in marriage. My concept of submission was "I'm so glad that I'm a guy!" I thought because I was the man, when I said "Frog," Brenda was supposed to jump. Not so according to Gary and the Bible. Before the Bible says, "Wives should submit to their husbands" (Eph. 5:24), it says, "Submit to one another out of reverence for Christ" (v. 21). Then husbands are told to love their wives "as Christ loved the church and gave himself up for her" (v. 25). That sounded like I needed to be willing to die for Brenda. Submission is to be the mutual attitude of the husband and the wife. When husbands and wives each have this attitude, they will have a God-honoring marriage. I'm glad I learned this lesson. Gary was the best man at my wedding. (As the groom, shouldn't I have been the best man?) Karolyn was also present.

Is there anyone in your life you could disciple—for life—the way Gary discipled me?

(Gary) In the earlier years, our friendship was a mentoring friendship. As Christians, we should always be seeking to mentor those who are younger than we. This is what Jesus meant when he said, "Therefore go and make disciples of all nations" (Matt. 28:19). What could be more important than investing your life in helping a younger person become a dedicated follower of Christ? But many of these mentoring friendships will develop into close personal friendships that last for a lifetime, in which we both learn from each other.

Look around your circles of influence—your family, workplace, church, and community. Look for someone you can mentor.

(Clarence) After Christina and Michelle, our twin girls, were born, Gary wrote this letter to them:

Dear Michelle and Christina:

I haven't met you yet, but I love you already because I have loved your mother and father for many years. You are very special children, and I hope that we can have a special relationship in the years ahead.

I pray that you will grow up to know and love Jesus

and invest your lives in serving him. I know that God will give each of you unique abilities. You are sisters and twins, but you are also individuals with different personalities and gifts, especially suited to do what God has in mind for your lives.

Many things will change in the world as you grow up, but God and his Word (the Holy Scriptures) will never change. Whenever you want to know the truth about something, you will always find it in the Bible. I will pray for you often, and for your parents that they will have wisdom in raising you. I know that they love you very much and want the best of everything for you.

Life will not always be easy, but it will always be meaningful if you follow God's way. Many years from now, when you are as old as I am, I hope that God will give you some special little girls whom you can love as I love you.

Gary, Karolyn, Shelley, and Derek all signed this letter to Christina and Michelle.

What an incredible blessing this letter was to Brenda and me, but also to our girls when we were able to read it to them. And it became more special when they could read it for themselves.

(Gary) As I read this letter again, tears come to my eyes as I look back and see how Christina, Michelle, and Andrea, who came later, have grown up to be Christ followers. They each have their own personalities and giftedness. But they are investing their lives in helping others. I have been greatly encouraged as I have observed God's hand in each of their lives. Their educational and vocational accomplishments bring me great joy. I know that in the years ahead, God will continue to use them to enrich the lives of many.

(Clarence) After Brenda gave birth to our twins, ten months later, we went to North Carolina. We wanted our family to see the girls. Our family included Karolyn and Gary. They took us to lunch. What I will never forget is this: as we approached the door to the restaurant, Gary took Christina out of my arms. He carried her with him into the restaurant, while Brenda, Karolyn, the other twin, Michelle, and I were waiting to be seated. Gary seemed to go to every table, interrupting people to tell them, "Look at my granddaughter!" These were mostly White people in this restaurant. They had the funniest looks of surprise on their faces seeing this White man parade this Black child through the restaurant and calling her his granddaughter. I looked at Karolyn. Karolyn is always cool. She said to me in her beautiful Southern accent, "Honey, this is his first grandchild!" Enough said. I was so honored that Gary and Karolyn considered us family. My girls consider them their grandparents. Gary and Karolyn financially supported the girls in college. .

Several times over the years, Gary has publicly said about me, "All that I have is his." It has been very humbling every time he has said this. For me, it translates that everyone I disciple has access to all of me. The same way Gary has invested in my life, I must invest in others. Investing deeply in others is a life-changing experience, not just for you but for your family members too.

(Gary) Well, I guess I acted a little crazy in the restaurant, but how do you expect a grandfather to act when he sees his first grandchild? After all, life's greatest meaning is found in relationships, first with God and then with friends. Is this not what true friendship is all about? We take what we have and make it available to each other. Our goal is to see each other flourish physically, emotionally, intellectually, and spiritually, all to the glory of God. When this happens, friendship has served its purpose.

(Clarence) Gary has been a part of every major decision I've ever made. For example, after touring with a Christian basketball team in Africa and Europe, I remember meeting with Mom and Gary to discuss the offer from a foreign country to become its women's head basketball coach. I wanted to do it, but to commit to only one year. That country wanted a two-year commitment. Neither Mom nor Gary would tell me what to do. They gave me options and consequences to prayerfully consider.

Gary has been with me through the good and bad. I'm sure there are many times that I've disappointed him. But we have always talked our way through our feelings. My love language is words of affirmation.[7] That is another insight about myself that I learned from Gary. What is so amazing to me is that in fifty-four years and counting, he has never said a negative word to me. That seems so impossible! He has never given up on me.

When I am back in my hometown for a visit, Gary and Karolyn's home is always open to me. Some of my fondest memories are of being in the kitchen and listening to Karolyn while she is making breakfast for me. She has so much wisdom! She is my favorite preacher, and no one else comes close.

Gary, his family, and the members of Calvary Baptist Church (where Gary attends) have made it impossible for me to say that all Whites are bad or prejudiced. I think most of us wrestle with prejudice, but it becomes less feasible when we develop close cross-cultural friendships.

(Gary) All of us are impacted by history—our own and that of our culture or race. So we often find ourselves with preconceived ideas about people of a different race or culture. These ideas might keep us apart unless we make an effort to get to know those who are different from us. That is why I believe the message of this book is so important. Once we develop a close cross-cultural friendship, we will likely change our preconceived ideas. We will begin to treat those who are different from

> Most of us wrestle with prejudice, but it becomes less feasible when we develop close cross-cultural friendships.

us with respect. Then we will likely develop additional friendships with those of a different race or culture. These may be different levels or types of friendships, but any level of friendship is a move in the right direction. Again I ask, what would happen in our country if every individual had at least one close personal friendship with someone of a different race or culture?

(Clarence) Knowing Gary definitely changed my worldview during turbulent times. Before meeting Gary and becoming a Christ follower, I planned to be an activist and join the Black Panthers after high school. I had never imagined being friends with a White man.

Now Gary's family has become mine. I deeply respect his daughter, Shelley; his son, Derek; and Shelley's children, Davy Grace and Elliott. I try to always send them a card on their birthdays, just a small way of saying, "I'm glad to be a part of your family."

John, Shelley's husband, really touched my heart on one of my visits to their home. John is like MacGyver, the main character of an old television show. I don't think there is anything he can't figure out! After I arrived at his home and got out of the car, John and another young man stopped their work in the yard. John introduced me to the young man by saying, "This is Shelley's brother." That meant so much to me! He did not say Shelley's Black brother, just her brother. I love being Black. But when John introduced me simply as Shelley's brother, the feeling of equality I had was inexpressible.

When I am in the state where they live, I make it a point to visit them. In 2019, I brought Brenda and our girls to this state because my older brother and several of my cousins live there. So naturally, one of our stops was Shelley's home. We took some family pictures together. After all, isn't that what families do?

Andrea, one of my daughters, said this about having Gary in her life:

> It's been an honor to have the well-known Dr. Gary Chapman in my life since birth! I've considered him to be a grandfather figure because I never knew my dad's father. Gary was around for my dad as a teen, and we've shared in each other's major life events ever since. Gary came to visit my sisters and me as babies. He came to my granny's funeral. We attended his daughter's wedding. I even skipped celebrating my twenty-first birthday with college friends to be present for the celebration of Gary's fortieth anniversary on

the staff of Calvary Baptist Church, which was happening the same weekend. I've always loved Grandpa Chapman and always will . . . race has never mattered.

Michelle wrote:

I never had the chance to meet my dad's father. He died when my dad was twenty. Despite that, I still grew up with a paternal grandfather. Gary Chapman came into my dad's life when he was a teen. Gary was the one who led my dad to Christ. He became a father figure to my dad and automatically became my grandfather. He has always been there for my sisters and me, and we always feel at home with him.

Gary has always loved and supported us in our goals and keeps tabs on what we are doing. To be able to see how much a part of my dad's life he's been and to see that continue with us has been a blessing. It doesn't matter that we aren't biologically related. Love is a choice you make day in and day out. Gary is a great representation of that, and I'm blessed he chose us to be a part of his family.

Christina said that writing about Gary was just too hard for her. She just could not put into words how she feels about him.

Yes, friends are friends forever. You too can have friendships that last a lifetime. Gary and Karolyn are those kind of friends to me and my family. We consider them family.

(Gary) Our daughter, Shelley, and son, Derek, have always considered Clarence a part of our family. They were young when Clarence started coming to our house every Friday night for our college gatherings. They expected him to show up every

Saturday morning for our time of Bible study. I think, even in those early years, they saw Clarence as a big brother. As they grew into adulthood, I was pleased to see that they continued to treat him as a brother. I see this as one of the reasons why both Shelley and Derek have always had positive relationships with people of different races or cultures. Cross-cultural friendships leave a positive legacy for generations to come.

Friendship is always a two-way street. When both individuals are listening to each other, they will both be learning. I have learned much from Clarence. My life would not have been the same without our friendship. To see him now as a husband, father, author, speaker, and disciple maker brings great joy to my heart. I have the sense that such lifelong friendships also bring joy to God.

> Cross-cultural friendships leave a positive legacy for generations to come.

Years ago, Michael W. Smith wrote a song titled "Friends." The chorus ends with the memorable line "a lifetime's not too long to live as friends." Clarence and I both love this song! It reminds us of the friendship God gave us, and of the kind of friendship we desire for others.

Your Thoughts

1. Do you have a person with whom you have been friends most of your life? If so, what has that been like for you?

2. If you have a best friend, how did you meet?

3. When you met, did you expect that you would be friends for so long?

4. What are key ingredients of your friendship?

5. What are some of the benefits of this long-term friendship for you?

6. What would you tell someone about how to maintain a friendship for a lifetime?

7. If you have had a cross-cultural friendship for a long time, how has it benefited your faith in Christ?

8. How has it influenced your ability to put yourself in someone else's situation and understand their perspective?

CHAPTER 9

Will You Accept Our Cross-Cultural Friendship Challenge?

At the fiftieth anniversary and retirement celebration for Dr. Gary and Karolyn Chapman, I saw people I hadn't seen in thirty, forty, and fifty years! All had returned to honor this godly couple. Gary did retire from being a staff member for Calvary Baptist Church, but he is not retiring from ministry.

This celebration was like a living yearbook of this church's members. People were hugging and taking pictures.

I was surprised by one of the White ladies who hugged me, because when she and I were seventeen, she never would have hugged me. She'd had a difficult time even speaking to me. Our initial relationship had been a challenge. But I had ministered to people in her family.

But on this special night, Gary, Karolyn, and I saw some of

the rewards of our embracing the challenge of a cross-cultural friendship. God used Gary and Karolyn to bring people of different cultures together for God's glory.

Here I was—not only me but my wife and daughters—being showered with love and affirmation primarily by Whites who had invested in my life when I was a teenager, a college student, and then later in ministry. God's love clearly had transcended (not eliminated) all of our cultural and racial differences. What a special night it was! Some said it was a glimpse of heaven.

But initiating and developing mutually beneficial, lifelong cross-cultural friendships isn't always easy.

After this celebration, several older White men in this church asked to have a relationship with me. One is reading my book *Winning the Race to Unity: Is Racial Reconciliation Really Working?* He said that he is surprised that he is loving it. He told me that he was initially fearful to read it because he thought the book would make him feel guilty for being White. This has led us to have more conversations. These conversations are honest and sometimes uncomfortable, but they are motivated and empowered by the love of Jesus Christ.

This relationship is happening now because of Gary's and my relationship.

If you have read to this point, hopefully you are open to the possibility of developing a friendship with someone of a different race or culture. Maybe you are saying, "But how?" Perhaps you are thinking, "I don't even have close friends within my own culture." If this is true, the idea of having a friendship with someone unlike you might seem like an impossible dream. In the New Testament book of Matthew, we read, "Jesus looked at them intently and said, 'Humanly speaking, it is impossible. But with God everything is possible'" (Matt. 19:26 NLT). So we are asking you not to begin this journey alone but rather to put your hand in God's hand and trust him with what happens.

We believe strongly that God wants all of his children to build friendships across racial and cultural lines. Near the end of his earthly life, Jesus gave his disciples a challenge. "Jesus came and told his disciples, 'I have been given all authority in heaven and on earth. Therefore, go and make disciples of *all the nations*, baptizing them in the name of the Father and the Son and the Holy Spirit. Teach these new disciples to obey all the commands I have given you. And be sure of this: I am with you always, even to the end of the age'" (Matt. 28:18–20 NLT, emphasis added). It is clear that we are to include people of other races. How can we as his disciples possibly rise to this challenge without having close relationships with people of other cultures? Again, please note, God is with us in this journey. We do not accomplish this in our own power. But he will give us the ability to do what he has commanded us to do. Not all friendships are discipleship friendships. But we want all of our friends to come to know and follow Christ.

It seems logical that the first step we need to take in our attempt to make cross-cultural friendships is to pray. Talk to God about your honest thoughts and feelings. Acknowledge your failures and ask for his wisdom and guidance as you open yourself to the possibility of building a friendship with someone of a different race. The apostle John said, "We are confident that he hears us whenever we ask for anything that pleases him. And since we know he hears us when we make our requests, we also know that he will give us what we ask for" (1 John 5:14–15 NLT). He will indeed enable us to do what he has asked us to do. He will open our eyes to possibilities that we have never before considered if we are asking for his guidance.

The second step in developing cross-cultural friendships is to seek to be a friendly person. Some people are by nature more outgoing than others. But all of us can develop the pattern of being friendly—being friendly minded, treating people as we would treat them if they were already a friend.

The First Two Steps for a Cross-Cultural Friendship

1. Pray.	"We are confident that he hears us whenever we ask for anything that pleases him" (1 John 5:14–15 NLT).
2. Seek to be a friendly person.	"A man who has friends must himself be friendly" (Prov. 18:24 NKJV).

(Clarence) Here is an example of how being friendly led to a friendship. Scott, who is Caucasian, is planting a church in a Southern state. He shared with me how he became friends with an African American man. They met while pumping gas. Scott was driving a minivan. He'd much prefer to be driving a truck. He noticed the African American man was also driving a minivan. According to Scott, he believed driving a minivan was definitely playing with their manhood just a little bit.

Scott told the African American how nice his minivan looked. The man replied, "It's not my favorite vehicle, but we've got five children and one on the way. So it's practical." Scott, a father of four, agreed.

They did not exchange phone numbers, but because Scott knew the African American man's job, he was able to find his information and give him a call. They met for lunch. They discovered that they both were Christians. They are now developing a friendship.

Scott models the biblical principle of being friendly: "A man who has friends must himself be friendly" (Prov. 18:24 NKJV).

How would you evaluate yourself as a friendly person? You might want to ask your family members to help you evaluate this. Ask people at your church, and possibly your peers at school and at work. Don't allow your personality to control your attitude and behavior toward others. Ask God to help you develop the trait of being friendly toward everyone you encounter.

> Ask God to help you develop the trait of being friendly toward everyone you encounter.

(Gary) One way to develop the trait of being friendly is to initiate conversations. Remember in chapter 3, the friendship that began in the grocery store where the two ladies, one was African American and the other was Caucasian, kept seeing each other week after week? Finally, one of them took a risk and initiated a conversation. The next week, there was another conversation. Step by step they became close friends and both of their lives were enriched.

To initiate a conversation with someone you do not know will not come naturally for a person who is an introvert. But if we are thinking and praying that God will lead us in developing a cross-cultural friendship, we can do what does not come naturally for us. The second conversation will come more easily than the first, and if it leads to a friendship, conversation will flow freely between the two of you. Not all conversations will lead to a friendship, but no friendship will ever develop without that initial conversation.

An important part of conversation is learning to ask questions and listen to the person's answers. This is the way we get to know another person. If we show a genuine interest in their story, most people will freely share. It is when we listen with empathy that they come to trust us and enjoy being with us. Think about the last time someone sincerely asked you, "What's going on in your life?" and then listened intently to what you shared. How did that make you feel? We tend to be drawn to people who express a sincere interest in our lives.

Another way to transform yourself into a friendly person,

How to Grow into a Friendlier Person

- Do not allow your personality to control your behavior toward others. (Ask God to develop a new friendly trait in you.)
- Initiate conversation with someone you do not know. (And for introverts, pray for God's leading.)
- Learn to ask questions and really listen to the person's answers.
- Show kindness to others in words and deeds.

or to become friendlier than you normally are, is to show kindness to others in words and deeds. An attitude of kindness is living with the desire to help people, to enrich their lives.

(Clarence) Brenda and I were on the road to a destination in Colorado to celebrate our thirty-fifth wedding anniversary. We made a pit stop to get gas and to switch drivers. While at this stop, I was shocked to see a truck driver back his truck into an extremely narrow parking spot between two cars. On my way back to our Jeep, I saw him in his truck preparing to leave. I waved my hand for him to stop. I approached him and said, "I saw you parking your truck. You were pretty impressive!" He smiled and replied, "I've been doing this for a minute." It was so much fun putting a smile on his face.

Afterward, I thought maybe with my being Black and his being White, my comment would make a difference in his next encounter with someone of a different culture. It took very little effort to say something nice. Kind words always create a more positive atmosphere. Accept the challenge and start looking for opportunities to say something positive and put a smile on someone's face, especially if that person is of a different culture or race. It might not lead to a friendship, but it will certainly create goodwill. Speaking kind words tends to stimulate others to speak kind words. Also, speaking kind words makes you feel better about yourself.

Kindness can also be expressed in deeds. Andrea Shuler shared the following experience. "Recently, I took a new job and moved into a new community. Several of my neighbors and colleagues at school gave me gifts. Some brought me meals, 'just because.' Others sent me money. I don't consider myself to be a charity case, but I accepted these gifts as expressions of love. Later, a few families invited me into their homes for holiday meals, celebrated my birthday, and invited me to their family outings. They were treating me as a friend, even though we were only recently acquainted. Perhaps in the future, we may truly become friends." How might you show kindness to someone who has recently moved into your neighborhood?

A person who has an attitude of kindness is looking for ways to serve or help others. Remember, Jesus said about himself, "The Son of Man came not to be served but to serve others and to give his life as a ransom for many" (Matt. 20:28 NLT). As we follow his model, we create an atmosphere in which friendships can be birthed.

(Gary) Recently I was in the checkout line to pay for a postcard. An African American gentleman was in front of me. When I got to the counter, the lady said, "The gentleman in front of you paid for your card." I said, "Really? What a nice man." I was eager to get outside and thank him, but by the time I got out the door, he was gone. I felt like I had missed an opportunity to make a new friend. His act of kindness made me want to get to know him. That is the power of acts of kindness.

The Things We Wish Everyone Knew

(Clarence) My friend Bev, who is White, said to me recently, "Many Whites feel guilty and ashamed for how Blacks have been treated." She also said that "many Whites don't know what to do." I was so moved by that. I thought, "I wish all Blacks knew that many Whites feel like that." I found Bev's comment confirmed by a White pastor of a megachurch, who confessed to two of his Black church members, "This racial tension [in our country] is bothering me, but I don't know what to do. Thank you for coming to me." The pastor took steps to improve diversity in his church after these two Black men met with him to gently discuss their concerns. And the pastor had these two men lead the staff of this megachurch in an eight-week biblical diversity Bible study.

We believe the road to greater understanding is through personal friendships. So we want to encourage Whites to keep attempting to initiate cross-cultural friendships. Don't worry about possibly being rejected, and don't take it personally should you be rejected.

On the other hand, many African Americans tend to struggle with trusting Whites because of the fear of being hurt in some way. We encourage African Americans to be patient with Whites. Be open to developing friendships. Whites are probably more open to developing friendships now than ever before. Don't judge all Whites by some negative experience you have had in your past.

Make Cross-Cultural Friendships Part of Your Normal Life

So where do cross-cultural friendships typically begin? In the normal flow of life. As we discussed earlier, almost all of us interface with people of another race on a regular basis. Much of the time, we simply ignore each other. But what would happen if we made an effort to get to know each other? We believe that many meaningful friendships would develop. Some of them could become lifelong friendships. Others might be temporary, but our lives would be greatly enriched.

(Clarence) Some friendships begin through sports. One of my White friends, whom I cherish, is a guy named Denny. We met when I would sneak into Wake Forest's gym to play basketball. I was fourteen and he was thirteen. We are still friends today. We don't talk often because we live in different states, but there is a special bond between us. One of my mentors said that we are close because we went to war together against racism. But we were not trying to fight racism. We were just demonstrating that Blacks and Whites can be friends. Just five years after the Civil Rights Act was passed, Denny and his other White friends were playing with Russell and me in the Black YMCA in the Black community. They were met with resistance but persevered and won the respect of the young and older men in the Black community. This experience bonded Denny and me for life. It was our love for sports that brought us together, but it was how we treated each other that built our friendship.

It was also sports that brought Gary and me together. I loved basketball and he loved people. Gary and I both mentioned that we never anticipated creating a friendship that has become more like family and that has lasted a lifetime. We just happened to be in the same place at the same time. Gary took the first step simply by being polite and kind. He treated us with respect, and in time we got to know each other. Though we did not set out to develop a friendship, we both were friendly toward each other. It is the choice to treat another as though they were a friend that leads to genuine friendship. When we become friendly to someone of a different culture, we plant the seeds of friendship.

(Gary) Because our friendship has so greatly enriched both of our lives, we want you to experience the benefits of cross-cultural relationships. That is what motivated us to write this book. In many ways, our culture seems more divided than in the 1960s, when our friendship began. We believe that will change only when individuals become friends with those of a different race. This is not only a challenge to Whites and Blacks. It is a challenge to people of all races and cultures. As we said in the introduction of this book, none of us chose our place of birth nor our race or culture. We are all known and loved by God equally. We need to love each other as God loves us. If this happens, we will find understanding and learn to work together for the benefit of all. We will transform culture one friendship at a time.

> We will transform culture one friendship at a time.

As Christians, we must take the lead. That does not mean that non-Christians cannot have meaningful friendships. They certainly can. But Christians not only have Christ's teachings and example but also have the power of Christ. The apostle Paul said, "God's love has been poured out into our hearts through the Holy Spirit" (Rom. 5:5). He also said, "I can do everything through Christ, who gives me strength" (Phil. 4:13 NLT). Again, we ask, what would happen in our nation, or any nation, if every Christian had at least one close friendship with someone of a different race or culture? We believe that it would radically change the world in which we live. So will you take the challenge and with God's help seek to begin a friendship with someone of a different race or culture in the coming year?

Your Thoughts

1. What suggestions would you give to help someone make cross-cultural friends?
2. Does the idea of trying to make a friend cross-culturally make you nervous? Why? Typically, feeling nervous about initiating a friendship even within your own culture is very normal.
3. What are some of the factors that make you nervous about initiating a friendship, whether it is cross-cultural or not?
4. If you are a Christ follower, how did reading the fact that nothing is impossible with God make you feel as you think about making a friend cross-culturally?
5. If you are a Christ follower, how did reading Matthew 28:18–20, the Great Commission that our Lord gave his disciples, make you feel about seeking cross-cultural friendships?
6. Have you ever thought about praying that God would give you a friend of another race? Will you consider praying for that now?
7. What role do you think your faith will play in making friends cross-culturally?

8. Do you consider yourself a friendly person? Would the people who know you best say the same?

9. If you don't consider yourself to be friendly, do you think the suggestions in this chapter will help you to become more friendly? Why or why not?

Acknowledgments

We would like to express our appreciation to the individuals who shared their stories of cross-cultural friendships with us. Also, we would like to thank Dylan Schlesinger, Webster Younce, Andy Rogers, Alicia Kasen, and the entire team at HarperCollins Christian Publishing and Zondervan for their help in making this book a reality. We are also deeply grateful for Jeff Wright and the team at Urban Ministries, who have helped greatly in the distribution of this book.

We would like to thank Jerald January, the catalyst who introduced HarperCollins Christian and Zondervan and Urban Ministries to our book project. We are also especially grateful to Andrea Shuler, Clarence's daughter, for her writing contribution to this book.

Last, but certainly not least, I (Clarence) am so indebted to Brenda, my wife, who allowed me some time away from her to write this book, and to Karolyn Chapman, who did the initial editing of the book. And I'm grateful for a little help from our friend Jerry Jenkins.

Notes

1. Daniel Cox, Juhem Navarro-Rivera, and Robert P. Jones, "Race, Religion, and Political Affiliation of Americans' Core Social Networks," Public Religion Research Institute, August 3, 2016, https://www.prri.org/research/poll-race-religion-politics-americans-social-networks/.

2. These six steps are excerpted from Clarence's book *Winning the Race to Unity: Is Racial Reconciliation Really Working?* (Chicago: Moody, 2003).

3. Gary Chapman and Jennifer Thomas, *The Five Languages of Apology: How to Experience Healing in All Your Relationships* (Chicago: Northfield Publishing, 2022).

4. Unlimited creativity is available to groups that are diverse. *Fortune* magazine annually rates and honors the top one hundred companies for their diversity efforts. Fortune 500 companies have shown that they must be diverse to compete for global dollars. We experience unlimited creativity when diverse people work together.

5. Quoted in Martin N. Davidson, "Know Thine Adversary: The Impact of Race on Styles of Dealing with Conflict," *Sex Roles: A Journal of Research* 45, nos. 5–6 (September 1, 2001): 259–76.

6. Martin Davidson, "Know Thine Adversary: The Impact of Race on Styles of Dealing with Conflict," *Sex Roles: A Journal of Research* 45, nos. 5–6 (September 1, 2001): 259–76.

7. Gary Chapman, *The Five Love Languages* (Chicago: Northfield Publishing, 1992).

Urban Ministries, Inc. (UMI), is one of the nation's oldest and most well-known Christian-resource providers to the African American church, serving thousands of churches over its fifty-year history with books, curriculum, small-group study resources, and vacation Bible school products. This book is published as part of a partnership between UMI and HarperCollins Christian Publishing.